How To Become The Best Of Men And Access The Best Of Life: From Ordinationary To Exceptional The Path Of Men Who Thrive. Vol 2

2, Volume 2

Thomas Mills

Published by Thomas Mills, 2024.

While every precaution has been taken in the preparation of this book, the publisher assumes no responsibility for errors or omissions, or for damages resulting from the use of the information contained herein.

HOW TO BECOME THE BEST OF MEN AND ACCESS THE BEST OF LIFE: FROM ORDINATIONARY TO EXCEPTIONAL THE PATH OF MEN WHO THRIVE. VOL 2

First edition. August 19, 2024.

Copyright © 2024 Thomas Mills.

ISBN: 979-8227608673

Written by Thomas Mills.

Also by Thomas Mills

Table of Contents

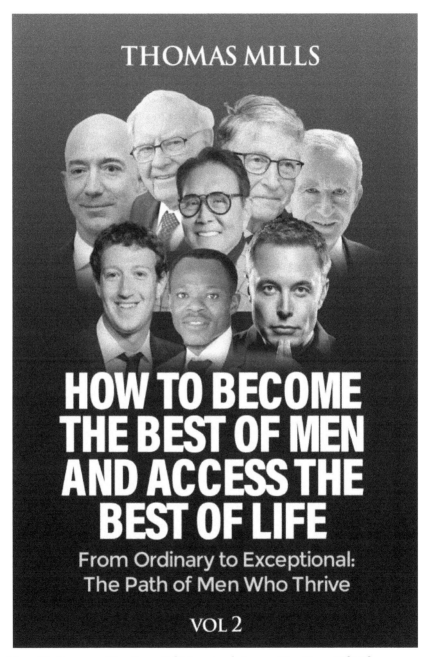

THOMAS MILLS

HOW TO BECOME THE BEST OF MEN AND ACCESS THE BEST OF LIFE

From Ordinary to Exceptional:
The Path of Men Who Thrive

VOL 2

How To Become The Best Of Men And Access The Best Of Life:
From Ordinationary To Exceptional

1

The Path Of Men Who Thrive
Vol 2
Thomas Mills

Part I

Foundation of Excellence

Chapter 1
The Power of Purpose

A s we explore "The Power of Purpose," inspired by Ellon Musk's visionary spirit and the innate wisdom of our surroundings, I will lead you on a transforming journey in this chapter. This ground-breaking chapter reveals seven game-changing techniques that will enable you to reach your full potential and live a meaningful, impactful life. Prepare to be inspired, encouraged, and empowered to set out on a path of meaning and purpose beyond anything you have ever experienced, drawing inspiration from the tenacity of nature and Elon Musk's inventive thinking.

Seven Nature-Inspired Methods to Reach Your Full Potential

1 . Clarity of vision

The stars shine brightly in the vastness of the cosmos, each with its own distinct path and purpose. Establish a clear direction for your life that is consistent with your core beliefs and objectives to fully embrace the power of visionary clarity. Let your vision lead you through the difficulties and unknowns, illuminating the way to your final goal, much like a star traverses the cosmos.

2. Adaptability during Adversity

With its robust roots, the majestic oak tree remains steady even during violent storms. Develop resilience as a cornerstone to support you on your path to meaning. Accept hardship as a chance for development and change, just as the oak tree endures the most trying circumstances. Allow resilience to serve as the cornerstone around which your aspirations are constructed, and use unshakable drive to overcome setbacks.

3. fervent pursuit

Passion flames bright in a volcano's molten core, igniting the unwavering drive toward creation and transformation. Kindle your passion and allow it to drive you toward your goals with boundless vigor and excitement. Let your passion shape your path, filling every step with purpose and zeal, just as a volcanic eruption shapes the landscape.

4. Community Partnership

Every plant and animal in the complex web of a forest ecosystem is essential to maintaining the peace among all of the others. Make relationships with people who share your vision and beliefs in order to build a community that will support and inspire you while you travel. As you work toward your goal, rely on your community for support and cooperation, just as the interwoven roots of a forest do.

5. Adaptive Quickness

The dolphin moves quickly and gracefully through its habitat while the tides of the ocean change constantly. Accept the fact that flexibility is essential to surviving in a world that is always changing. Be resilient and adaptable as you turn toward new chances, learn from your mistakes, and face obstacles with the same agility of a dolphin.

6. Impactful Service

A butterfly's delicate touch, while pollinating flowers, embodies the transformational potential of impact and service. Discover contentment in helping others and changing the world for the better. Let your actions spread compassion like a butterfly extending its wings, encouraging everyone around you to live a life with meaning and purpose.

7. Eternal Legacy

Towering giants bear witness to the enduring legacy of purpose and vision in the ancient groves of the redwoods. Seize the chance to create a legacy that is ageless and will inspire wonder and astonishment for years to come. Allow your deeds of today to create a legacy that will last forever, one that is replete with inspiration, hope, and knowledge.

Identifying The Purpose Of Your Life

You can use the following strategies to figure out what your life's purpose is:

1. Seeing Clearly: Adoring Your North Star

For sailors traversing the oceans, the North Star serves as a beacon of guidance in the vastness of the night sky. Similarly, develop visionary clarity by discovering your personal North Star, which is a distinct and alluring vision that directs you toward your mission. In the same way that Elon Musk's vision drove him to transform entire industries, let your North Star motivate and guide you on your path to a fulfilling and influential life.

Finding your life's mission starts with developing visionary clarity, much like Elon Musk did when his unflinching vision allowed him to transform entire industries. Find your personal North Star, a dazzling, unmistakable light that points the way to success. Allow this vision to drive and inspire you, directing each choice you make and action you take to realize your life's ultimate goal.

2. Adversity-Resilient - Grounded Like the Mighty Oak

Develop resilience to get through the obstacles and disappointments you face on the way to your purpose, much like the strong oak tree does when it faces the worst of the weather. Take courage from the deep roots of the oak tree and establish a strong foundation of tenacity and resolve. Recall that hardship serves as a springboard for development and transformation rather than the destination, enabling you to come out stronger and more resilient than before.

Take courage from the tenacity of well-known individuals like Jeff Bezos when faced with difficulties. Accept hardship as a force for change and development that will help you develop tenacity and unflinching resolve. Consider setbacks as chances to grow and become stronger, more resilient, and closer to achieving your life's mission, much like a phoenix emerging from the ashes.

3. Enthusiastic Interest - Kindling the Fire Within

Passion flames fiercely at the center of a blazing wildfire, providing unwavering energy and tenacity. Accept your inner fire and allow it to fuel your ardent and enthusiastic pursuit of your goal. Make sure that every move you take in your pursuit of your ultimate goals is driven by unrelenting focus and commitment by channeling the enthusiasm of visionaries such as Jeff Bezos.

Embrace the unrestrained passion and tenacity that drive visionary leaders on their journey towards purpose. Allow your enthusiasm and steadfast dedication to carry you forward by letting your passion be the driving force behind your efforts. Use the unwavering pursuit of purpose exhibited by prosperous people to kindle a fire inside of you and move you closer to your real calling.

4. Community Involvement – Building Your Support Network

Create deep connections with people who encourage and inspire you on your meaningful journey, just as interconnected ecosystems flourish in the natural world. Embrace a community that shares your beliefs and vision and offers accountability, support, and encouragement. Take a cue from Elon Musk about how to create lasting connections that encourage creativity and teamwork in the pursuit of a larger goal.

As with Elon Musk, surround yourself with people who inspire and support you, who hold you accountable and offer accountability. Build a tribe of people who share your vision and work together to achieve common objectives. This will create a network of support that will enable you to grow and achieve your goals.

5. Adjustable Flexibility - Handling Transition with Style

The dolphin moves through shifting waters with agility and elegance as the tides come in and out. Accept adaptable agility as a fundamental quality in your quest of meaning, as it will enable you to deal with adversity and change with fortitude and adaptability. Adopt an attitude of constant learning and adjustment, imitating the ability to seize opportunities in the face of change exhibited by great businesspeople like Warren Buffett.

Utilize the astute strategic flexibility exhibited by prosperous businessmen such as Warren Buffett to grasp possibilities amid change. Adopt an attitude of constant learning and development, which will enable you to adapt to changing circumstances and prosper on your path to fulfilling your life's mission.

6. Service with Impact: Establishing a Durable Trajectory

Find joy in helping others and having a beneficial influence on the world around you, much like the soft touch of a pollinating bee. Accept a life of meaningful service where your deeds bring about transformation and change in others. Continue the legacy of positive change and transformation established by philanthropic visionaries such as Bill Gates, whose dedication to meaningful giving has left a lasting legacy.

Serving others and having a positive impact on the world around you can bring you fulfillment. Make sure that your actions are in line with a larger purpose in order to leave a lasting legacy of positive change and transformation that touches others and goes beyond personal fulfillment.

7. Eternal Legacy: Creating Your Lasting Influence

See the enduring heritage of purpose and vision engraved in the fabric of nature as you stand beneath the towering redwoods, which stand like titans of time. Imagine the kind of legacy you want to leave behind—one that inspires and endures across time for future generations. Seize every moment as a chance to mold an enduring legacy of meaning, influence, and motivation by emulating the innovative and transformative spirit of visionary leaders such as Richard Branson.

Leave a lasting legacy that will inspire upcoming generations and leave a lasting impression on the globe. As you construct a timeless legacy that endures through the centuries and solidifies your position as a catalyst for positive change and transformation, embody the spirit of invention, purpose, and resilience.

Putting Purpose Into Your Actions

Greetings from a transforming guide that helps you connect your activities with your purpose in order to achieve success and fulfillment. With inspiration from the lives of the wealthiest and most visionary people on the planet, including Elon Musk and other well-known personalities, "Purpose Aligned" provides a road map for realizing your own potential and making a remarkable impact. Accept the power of purpose and set out on a path that goes beyond achievement to build a meaningful and purposeful existence.

1. Light Up Your Way with Meaning

Accept the unwavering vision that characterizes great leaders such as Elon Musk. Ensure that everything you do is guided by a distinct goal that will help you make wise decisions in all that you do. Allow your mission to illuminate your path and motivate uncompromising dedication to your goals, just as Musk's vision catapulted SpaceX and Tesla to previously unheard-of heights. Your biggest goals will become a reality when your actions are in line with your mission and every move you take is deliberate.

2. Build Strength in the Battlefield of Difficulties

Take inspiration from the tenacity of the richest people on the planet, like Jeff Bezos, who overcame adversity to achieve success. Align your activities with your mission by seeing obstacles as chances for development and change. Accept adversity as a source of resilience, generating the will to keep going when things get tough. Let adversities strengthen your commitment to align your actions with purpose and emerge stronger than ever, just as Bezos used Amazon's hardship to spur innovation.

3. Drive Your Path with Unwavering Enthusiasm

Bring the ferocious fire that visionary leaders like Richard Branson possess to your actions. Align your quest with your mission by bringing boundless zeal and devotion to your travels. Allow your passion to be the motivation behind your activities and the unrelenting devotion that will carry you towards your goals. Draw inspiration from the unwavering pursuit of goals exhibited by accomplished people to bring passion and purpose to all that you do.

4. Build Growth-Oriented Supportive Networks

To emulate philanthropists such as Bill Gates, engage with your community and use it to connect your activities with a cause. Embrace a tribe of people who share your values and who will encourage and support your vision. Develop connections with others who share your beliefs and motivate you to pursue your goals. Create a network that encourages growth and cooperation as you synchronize your activities with your mission, just as Gates did by leveraging community support to bring about significant change.

5. Handle Change with Strategic Agility

Accept the flexibility that successful businesspeople like Warren Buffett have embraced to be purposeful in the face of shifting circumstances. Cultivate an adaptable and learning mindset that enables you to change course and grab opportunities. Strategic flexibility is necessary to match your actions to your goals and allow you to move through uncertainty with grace and accuracy. Accept change as a driving force for personal development and evolution as you pursue your goals.

6. Generate a Significant Change Ripple

Answer the invitation to live a purpose-driven life by imitating the charitable pursuits of prosperous visionaries and adopting a life of impact and service. Discover contentment in helping others and changing the world in a significant way. Make sure your actions are in line with a bigger purpose that goes beyond your own interests in order to leave a lasting legacy of transformation and improvement. In the same way that charitable icons have changed the world for the better by serving others, match your efforts to a cause that will have a lasting effect.

7. Create a Lasting Impact

Think about the lasting influence of global visionaries and the legacy you hope to leave behind. To leave a lasting legacy that spans generations, make sure your actions are in line with your intentions. Write a story that will be remembered for its inventiveness, determination, and purpose—one that will leave a lasting impression on the world. When your actions are in line with your mission, each activity will make a lasting and meaningful contribution to the legacy.

Chapter 2
Unleashing Your Potential

I'm excited to take you on a life-changing trip to realize your full potential in this chapter, which is inspired by the true stories of the wealthiest geniuses on the planet. We explore the tactics and mentalities that have driven well-known people to extraordinary success, such as Elon Musk, Jeff Bezos, and other prominent characters, in this engrossing manual. Learn seven crucial strategies to reach your full potential by taking inspiration from the experiences of others who have forged paths for impact, resilience, and creativity. Get ready to take a journey that will not only increase your success but also have a worldwide impact through enduring legacy.

1. Your Goal with Accuracy

Accept the visionary leadership of trailblazers such as Elon Musk. Define your purpose with clarity and unrelenting focus to unlock your potential. Align your actions with a distinct and compelling purpose that motivates audacious action and steadfast dedication, much as Musk's vision inspired him to disrupt industries with SpaceX and Tesla. Allow your vision to serve as the driving force that, with deliberate and strategic clarity, moves you closer to your goals.

2. Survive in the Face of Adversity

Take inspiration from the fortitude of Jeff Bezos and other business titans who overcame hardship to achieve success. Develop resilience as a pillar of your quest to unlock your potential. Instead of seeing obstacles as failures, see them as chances for development and improvement. To emulate Bezos's successful transformation of failures into opportunities for innovation at Amazon, strengthen your will to overcome challenges with poise and tenacity. Accept hardship as a growth-promoting force that will increase your ability to persevere and achieve success.

3. Activate Your Motivation with a Passionate Purpose

Bring the ferocious enthusiasm of innovators like Richard Branson to your path. Your activities must be driven by sincere passion and steadfast determination if you want to reach your full potential. Allow your enthusiasm to be the engine that will push you with unwavering vigor and energy to achieve your goals. Draw inspiration from the fervent quest of purpose exhibited by accomplished people to imbue each undertaking with significance, influence, and satisfaction.

---

4. CREATE NETWORKS That Will Encourage Growth

Take charitable giants like Bill Gates' lead and value the importance of community connections. Surround yourself with a network of like-minded people that encourage and motivate you on your journey to fully realize your potential. Build connections with people who share your values and goals in order to promote cooperation, development, and assistance to one another. Create a network that supports your mission and increases your influence, just as Gates did by leveraging community support to bring about significant change.

5. Adapt to Change with Strategic Swiftness

Accept the flexibility that successful businesspeople like Warren Buffett have shown. Develop a flexible and strategically agile attitude that will allow you to navigate change with confidence and accuracy in order to fully realize your potential. Adopt a purposeful mindset by viewing change as a chance for creativity and development. React quickly to changing conditions, grab chances, and change course quickly to maintain an advantage in your quest for success.

6. Take Action with a Purpose to Change Things

Embrace a life of impact and service to align your actions with meaning. Take inspiration from the charitable pursuits of accomplished visionaries. To reach your full potential, discover fulfillment in helping others and making a significant impact on the world. Allow a higher purpose to direct your activities instead of just self-interest, so that you might leave a legacy of transformation and good influence. In the same way that charitable icons have changed society for the better by serving others, match your actions to a cause to bring about significant change.

7. Develop a Lasting Impact

Think about the lasting influence of global visionaries and the legacy you hope to leave behind. To reach your full potential and leave a lasting legacy that inspires future generations, match your actions with your purpose. Create a story that is innovative, meaningful, and has a lasting effect on the world. Make certain that each project helps to create a legacy that is significant and long-lasting, influencing a legacy that is not limited by time or location.

Seven Techniques For Recognizing And Leveraging Your Special Talents

1. Light Up Your Way with Clarity

Clarify your passions, interests, and innate talents to start the process of discovering your own strengths. Follow your natural talents and hobbies to create a successful route, just like IT sector innovators like Mark Zuckerberg did with their coding expertise. Find the things that make you unique and give you a sense of purpose so that you can pursue chances that will allow you to shine brightly and have a significant effect.

2. Accept Individuality and Authenticity

Accept who you really are and cherish the things that set you apart from the crowd. Be motivated by role models such as Oprah Winfrey, who established a media empire by using her storytelling skills and genuineness. By remaining loyal to who you are and embracing your uniqueness, you open up a world of unrealized potential and create the conditions for unmatched achievement. Being true to who you are generates opportunities that play to your strengths and builds real relationships that help you reach new heights.

3. Develop a Growth Mentality

Encourage a growth mentality, which is based on resilience, ongoing learning, and progress. Take inspiration from someone like Jeff Bezos, who built Amazon into a worldwide powerhouse via his unwavering pursuit of innovation. You may fully utilize your abilities when you embrace a philosophy of constant improvement and see obstacles as chances for personal development. Develop a thirst for information, look for novel experiences, and view obstacles as opportunities to grow and advance.

4. Utilize Your Advantages

Determine your main advantages and use them to your advantage in every area of your life. Take an example from Warren Buffett, who leveraged his astute investment sense to amass enormous riches. Concentrate on developing your abilities and using them to pursue worthwhile projects that complement your objectives and moral principles. You may increase your chances of success, fulfillment, and influence in all that you do by focusing on your strengths.

5. Seek Advice and Mentorship

Seek for mentorship from seasoned people who can offer insightful advice on how to best utilize your special talents. Take a cue from the relationship of mentorship between Warren Buffett and Bill Gates, where their mutual support and learning drove their success. Assemble a network of mentors that can push you to expand beyond your preconceived boundaries, share their wisdom, and provide constructive criticism. Taking advantage of mentorship can help you reach new heights of potential and accelerate your career and personal progress.

6. Create Strategic Alliances

Work together with people and groups that enhance your abilities and increase your influence. Consider fruitful collaborations such as the one between Larry Page and Sergey Brin, whose synergistic abilities facilitated the founding of Google. Establishing strategic partnerships with like-minded individuals broadens your reach, enhances your talents, and creates growth prospects. By forming strategic alliances, you may take advantage of everyone's resources and abilities to succeed and innovate at even higher levels.

7. Live Passionately for Your Purpose

Make the most of your abilities by combining them with a passion and purpose that will keep you motivated and ambitious. Draw motivation from Elon Musk, whose unwavering pursuit of his sustainable future vision has revolutionized various industries. Lead a purposeful life that is in line with your basic principles and convictions, giving each deed a sense of urgency and significance. By combining your abilities with a greater good, you can reach your full potential and leave a lasting legacy that goes beyond personal achievement.

How to Get Past Your Own Limitations

This section delves into the fundamental idea of breaking free from self-imposed restrictions, and I'm going to take you on a transformative journey towards self-discovery and empowerment. Inspired by the true stories of the wealthiest visionary and resilient people on the planet, this book provides a road map for escaping the chains of fear and self-doubt. Learn the critical techniques and insights that can catapult you into unmatched achievement, self-improvement, and freedom from the limitations preventing you from reaching your full potential.

1. Face Your Inner Critic

Put an end to the critical and self-doubting voice that prevents you from achieving your goals and aspirations. Seek inspiration from entrepreneurs such as Elon Musk, who overcame doubters and transformed industries with their audacious ideas. Reframe your negative beliefs, engage in self-compassion exercises, and accept failure as a chance for personal development to confront your inner critic. Liberate yourself from the constraints that your own thoughts have placed on you and develop a resilient, self-assured mindset.

2. Accept Fear and Take a Courageous Step

Fear does not equate to courage; rather, courage is the resolve to face fear head-on and press on in spite of it. Take inspiration from trailblazers like Jeff Bezos, who used risk and uncertainty to grow Amazon into a worldwide powerhouse. To achieve greater things, accept fear as a necessary component of growth, push yourself past your comfort zone, and move outside of it. You can break through the walls of your own self-imposed restrictions and discover a universe of unrealized potential by developing bravery and accepting challenges.

3. MAKE AUDACIOUS PLANS and move forward

Make a path free of self-imposed constraints by deciding on big, audacious goals that will encourage and inspire you. Take a cue from visionary leaders such as Steve Jobs, who propelled Apple to unparalleled success via his unwavering pursuit of excellence. By establishing specific goals, coming up with workable plans, and consistently moving toward your goals, you can escape mediocrity. Accept the ability of goal-setting to help you overcome limitations you place on yourself and advance toward greatness.

4. Foster Adaptability and Resilience

Resilience becomes your most valuable tool in conquering constraints that you place on yourself when faced with hardship and setbacks. Consider strong individuals such as Oprah Winfrey, who ascended from modest origins to become a prominent media personality and philanthropist. Develop resilience by viewing obstacles as chances for improvement, taking lessons from failures, and adjusting to change with poise and dexterity. You may overcome self-imposed constraints with every new challenge by cultivating a robust attitude that enables you to traverse hurdles with fortitude and perseverance.

5. Seek Guidance and Take Input from Others

Seek advice and mentorship from people who have already travelled the path you wish to take in order to break free from the constraints of self-imposed limitations. Take a cue from accomplished mentors such as Warren Buffett, whose advise and experience have influenced numerous financial techniques. Encircle yourself with mentors who can guide you on your path to self-realization and provide insightful advice, helpful criticism, and encouragement. You can acquire perspective, insight, and the means to overcome limitations that you have placed on yourself by accepting mentorship and learning from the experiences of others.

6. Encourage a spirit of growth and lifelong learning.

Adopt a growth attitude that depends on ongoing education, advancement, and change. Take a cue from visionary leaders like Mark Zuckerberg, who continuously innovated and adjusted to the rapidly changing digital industry. Liberate yourself from stuck attitudes by accepting difficulties, asking for feedback, and seeing setbacks as chances for improvement. One way to broaden your horizons and overcome self-imposed boundaries is to develop a voracious appetite for knowledge, welcome fresh viewpoints, and make a commitment to lifelong learning.

7. Possess Self-Belief and Accept Responsibility

The secret to overcoming self-imposed constraints is to have confidence in yourself and accept responsibility for your path. Consider self-made businesspeople like Richard Branson, who radiate conviction and confidence in all they do. Take responsibility for your decisions and deeds, have faith in your skills, and follow your gut. You give yourself the capacity to overcome the confines of self-imposed limitations and forge your own route to success and fulfillment by adopting self-belief and accountability.

Part II

Mindset Mastery

Chapter 3: Mastering The Growth Mindset

Chapter 4

Mental Toughness

Chapter 3
Mastering The Growth Mindset

E nter a world where achievement has no boundaries and those who are resilient and affluent use the Growth Mindset's transformational power to pave the way to greatness. This chapter delves into the lives of the wealthiest visionaries and luminaries on the planet to uncover priceless insights for developing a mindset that inspires people to achieve remarkable things. This part, which draws on profound ideas and real-life experiences, reveals the seven essential steps to adopting a growth mindset and opening the door to unmatched success. Come along on this life-changing trip with me, where the thinking of millionaires serves as your road map to a future full of fulfillment and boundless possibilities.

1. Take on Challenges with Passion

In the world of the extremely successful, difficulties are not barriers to achievement but rather stepping stones. Take inspiration from someone like Jeff Bezos, who turned Amazon from a little online bookshop into a major force in the world, and approach obstacles with passion and unyielding resolve. Change your mindset to see obstacles as chances for development and education, which will help you reach greater achievement with each obstacle you overcome.

2. Continue in the Face of Misery

The quality that distinguishes individuals who rise above mediocrity to greatness is resilience. Draw motivation from Oprah Winfrey's story of accomplishment overcoming poverty and achieving media mogul and charity icon status via her unshakable tenacity in the face of hardship. Develop a resilient mindset by persevering through failures, setbacks, and obstacles with the understanding that they are all just temporary detours on the path to achievement.

3. Ask for Input and Welcome Ongoing Improvement

The compass that directs the path to excellence is feedback. Take a cue from Warren Buffett, who ascended to the top of the financial industry by his unwavering dedication to seeking input and making constant improvements. Accept criticism as a useful tool for personal development and use the lessons you've learned from both achievements and setbacks to hone your abilities. Adopting a feedback-centric mindset opens the door to ongoing improvement and craft mastery.

4. See Failures as a Chance for Improvement

In the world of the extremely successful, failing is a necessary step on the path to mastery rather than a discouragement. Take Elon Musk as an example. Despite many losses in his daring endeavors, his development attitude and resilience have allowed him to transform entire sectors. Accept setbacks as chances for development and learning, from which you can glean important lessons and insights that fortify your resolve and redouble your efforts to succeed.

5. Develop an Intense Interest in Education and Creativity

Innovation is essential to success and advancement. Learn from Mark Zuckerberg's unwavering drive for innovation at Facebook, where he revolutionized social networking with his love of learning and pushing the envelope. Develop an innovative and inquisitive mentality that will allow you to be receptive to fresh perspectives and ideas that could revolutionize your work and lead you to unprecedented success.

6. Honor the Achievements of Others

The accomplishments of others serve as a source of inspiration and motivation rather than posing a danger in a world of prosperity and success. Take a cue from Richard Branson's humility and kindness, as he encourages teamwork and a collaborative atmosphere while acknowledging the accomplishments of others. Adopt a spirit of plenty and unity in which acknowledging the achievements of others inspires and motivates you to reach new heights of joy and success.

7. See Success and Move Strategically

Clear goals and a clear image of your desired outcome are the first steps towards success. Emulate Steve Jobs, whose astute decision-making and imaginative leadership made Apple a symbol of innovation. Clarity and precision in your visualization of success can help you set strategic goals and take consistent action to bring your ambitions to reality. You may fully realize the benefits of the Growth Mindset and take yourself to previously unheard-of levels of fulfillment and achievement by combining vision with action.

How to Develop Adaptability and Resilience

1 .Accept Change with Empathy
Change is not a threat in the fast-paced world of the ultra-successful; rather, it is a chance for development and evolution. Take a cue from Bill Gates, who skillfully and nimbly led Microsoft through significant changes in the technology industry. Adopt a mindset that thrives in the face of uncertainty and accepts new difficulties as stepping stones to excellence. Embrace change as a fuel for innovation and reinvention.

2. Create a Steely Will in the Face of Misery

Those who overcome adversity and come out stronger on the other side are built on resilience. Examine the unwavering determination of Jeff Bezos, whose unwavering persistence drove Amazon from modest origins to worldwide dominance. Develop a steely resolve in the face of difficulty by seeing obstacles as chances to strengthen your perseverance and resilience as you go toward unheard-of accomplishment.

3. Adapt to a Changing Environment and Succeed

The superpower that sets the exceptional apart from the common person is adaptability. Take inspiration from Warren Buffett's strategic acumen, which has solidified his reputation as an investment legend through his ability to adjust to shifting market conditions. Develop an agile and flexible attitude that allows you to quickly adjust to changing circumstances and grow stronger and more robust with each change.

4. Acknowledge Failures and Develop Resilience

Failures teach us to be resilient and strong, not to give up. Follow in Elon Musk's footsteps; his failures with SpaceX and Tesla served to strengthen his resolve to succeed. Accept failures as chances for personal development and education, drawing insightful lessons that fortify your fortitude and provide you the tools you need to face obstacles head-on in the future.

5. Invent and Develop with a Goal in Mind

Innovation is essential to advancement and flexibility. Draw inspiration from Mark Zuckerberg's imaginative leadership, as his unwavering drive for innovation at Facebook has completely changed the social media environment. Develop an enthusiasm for ongoing innovation and change, which will motivate you to adjust to new situations with a purpose and a vision that will catapult you into previously unheard-of levels of achievement.

6. Create a Network for Assistance and Cooperation

Being resilient requires teamwork and cooperation rather than being a solo endeavor. Observe Richard Branson's collaborative approach as he fosters a network of varied skills and viewpoints to lead Virgin Group to unprecedented heights. Create a network of cooperation and support by surrounding yourself with positive and motivating people who will help you weather difficult times together and come out stronger.

7. Seek Resilience and Move Strategically

The mental foundation of resilience is a clear belief in one's capacity to triumph over misfortune and prosper in the face of difficulties. Channel Steve Jobs' strategic vision. The company achieved unprecedented success because to Jobs' strategic moves and his unrelenting belief in Apple's potential. Imagine yourself being resilient with clarity and purpose, achieving new heights of success and fulfillment by defining strategic goals and acting decisively.

7 **Strategies for Viewing Difficulties as Possibilities**

I invite you to embark on a life-changing journey into the success realm in this part by viewing obstacles as opportunities. We'll reveal seven calculated approaches that are based on the actual experiences of the richest people and most powerful figures on the planet. From utilizing resilience in the face of difficulty to transforming setbacks into stepping stones, we reveal the secrets to unlocking your potential, seizing opportunities, and paving the way to unmatched success. Come along on this fascinating journey with me as we explore the life-changing potential of viewing obstacles as opportunities.

1. Recast difficulties as opportunities for development

In the world of the extremely successful, setbacks are opportunities for development and innovation rather than barriers. Take a cue from Jeff Bezos, who turned obstacles into chances for Amazon's rapid expansion, and discover how to reinterpret difficulties as opportunities for both career and personal growth. Accept every obstacle as an opportunity to push yourself beyond your comfort zone, realize your full potential, and achieve unmatched achievement.

———◉———

2. DEVELOP RESILIENCE Despite Misfortune

Those that flourish in the face of adversity are known for their resilience. Take a cue from the legendary position of Warren Buffett in the investment industry, which he has achieved via his unrelenting endurance in managing market changes. Develop resilience by taking on obstacles head-on, picking up lessons from mistakes, and getting back up stronger than before. Allow failures to serve as stepping stones to resilience, helping you achieve previously unheard-of levels of success.

3. Seek for Creativity When Things Change

Innovation flourishes in the face of difficulty and transition. The unrelenting quest of innovation by Mark Zuckerberg at Facebook provides a model for viewing obstacles as chances for development. Accept change as an opportunity for creativity and take advantage of it to shift course, adjust, and advance. Use your creativity to turn obstacles into chances that will help you reach new heights of achievement.

4. Use Focus and Determination

The motivation that helps people overcome obstacles and achieve their goals is determination. Elon Musk exemplifies the strength of endurance via his persistent focus and tenacity in the face of setbacks with SpaceX and Tesla. Use your willpower, remain committed to your objectives, and direct your energy on surmounting obstacles with unyielding resolve. Allow tenacity to be your driving force as you seize chances concealed by obstacles.

5. Create a Growth Support System

Collaboration is often necessary for success. Richard Branson's skill at creating a network of cooperation and support emphasizes how crucial it is to surround yourself with the right people. Create a network of support that fosters your development, offers direction when things become tough, and gives you the confidence to see setbacks as chances for both professional and personal improvement. Build a network that encourages and helps you succeed.

6. Use Failure as a Springboard for Success

Failure is a necessary step on the path to success rather than the end. As a teacher, accept failure, grow from your errors, and seize fresh chances. Taking a cue from Steve Jobs's journey, who at Apple converted mistakes into successes, use setbacks as teaching opportunities to propel yourself toward higher accomplishments. Accept challenges as chances to improve your abilities, think outside the box, and make plans for success.

7. Adopt a growth mindset and engage in ongoing education.

It takes a growth mentality to see obstacles as opportunities. The philosophy of continual improvement is personified by Bill Gates' dedication to perpetual learning and development. Adopt a growth mindset, look for opportunities to learn, and respond nimbly and curiously to obstacles. Develop an insatiable curiosity, welcome change, and capitalize on the potential of lifelong learning to turn obstacles into chances for development and achievement.

Chapter 4
Mental Toughness

I'd want to thank you for making it this far. Welcome to the world of mental toughness, a quality that the wealthiest people in the world admire for enabling them to overcome obstacles and achieve remarkable achievement. In this captivating chapter, we explore the fundamentals of mental toughness with firsthand accounts and wisdom from illustrious individuals who have used this quality to overcome hardship and reach the highest levels of success. Come along on a self-exploration adventure with me as we learn seven tactical strategies for developing mental toughness and unlocking the secrets of unmatched achievement.

1. Accept Misery as a Growth-Catalyst

Adversity is a springboard for resilience and personal development rather than a barrier. Take inspiration from people who have overcome adversity to become successful in the media, such as Oprah Winfrey, and learn to see obstacles as chances for growth on both a personal and professional level. Develop the mentality that challenges you to grow, pushes you beyond your comfort zone, and kindles the resilience fire within of you.

———◆———

2. GAIN UNWAVERING Self-Assurance in Your Capabilities

The foundation of mental toughness is confidence, which gives you the ability to face uncertainty head-on with unshakeable conviction. Take a cue from Elon Musk, who achieved extraordinary success via his unwavering faith in his ideas for SpaceX and Tesla. Gain a strong sense of confidence in your skills, follow your gut feeling, and project assurance when confronted with obstacles. Allow confidence to be your beacon of hope as you overcome challenges and realize greatness.

3. Develop Laser-Guided Observation

The motivation that propels people toward their objectives, despite enormous obstacles, is determination. Take a cue from Jeff Bezos, whose unwavering quest of Amazon's success revolutionized the e-commerce industry. Develop a laser-like focus, make specific goals, and stick to your course in the face of obstacles. Use your unwavering commitment as a guide to overcome challenges and fulfill your goals.

4. Accept Resilience When You Face Obstacles

The foundation of mental toughness is resilience, which enables people to overcome adversity and emerge stronger on the other side. Embrace resilience as a defense against misfortune, taking inspiration from the career of Warren Buffett, who persevered through market volatility with poise and determination. Recognize how to bounce back from losses, grow from mistakes, and become stronger and more resilient. Perceive failures as opportunities to strengthen your commitment and drive you toward unimaginable accomplishment.

5. Learn the Art of Stress Reduction

Although stress will always be a part of the journey to success, sustaining mental toughness requires learning how to manage it. Consider adopting Bill Gates' strategies, who places a high value on stress reduction and self-care despite his hectic schedule. Learn how to effectively handle stress by practicing self-care, mindfulness, and meditation. These practices will help you stay mentally strong and resilient when faced with obstacles.

6. Seek Advice and Mentoring to Promote Your Growth

To develop mental toughness and overcome obstacles with grace, mentoring and advice are priceless resources. Consider Richard Branson as an example, who looked to seasoned businesspeople for guidance while navigating the rough seas of entrepreneurship. Look for mentors that can uplift, mentor, and impart knowledge that fortifies your resolve and gives you the tools you need to face obstacles head-on and with grace.

7. Engage in self-reflection and ongoing development.

One of the best strategies for developing mental toughness and personal development is self-reflection. Take a cue from Mark Zuckerberg, who uses introspection to spur creativity and expansion at Facebook. Think critically, assess your advantages and disadvantages, and make a commitment to lifelong learning. Adopt a growth attitude that is fueled by self-awareness, flexibility, and an unwavering quest for perfection.

How to Become Resilient Despite Adversity

Welcome to a transforming voyage into the world of resilience—a quality that the wealthiest people on the planet admire for its transformative power to overcome hardship and emerge stronger than before. This section explores the fundamentals of resilience through firsthand accounts and analysis from notable individuals who have used this quality to overcome adversity and achieve previously unheard-of levels of achievement. Come along as we share seven tactical strategies for building resilience and discovering the secrets to facing hardship with grace and unshakeable fortitude.

1. Accept Misfortune as a Doorway to Development

Adversity is a bridge to personal and professional growth rather than a barrier. Take a cue from Jeff Bezos's career, where he turned obstacles into opportunities for Amazon's success, and learn to see obstacles as chances to strengthen your resilience and better yourself. Adopt the belief that hardship encourages development, sparks creativity, and drives you to new heights of success.

2. Develop Unwavering Self-Belief in Your Resilience

Resilience is built on confidence, which gives you the ability to traverse choppy waters with a steadfast belief in your capacity to overcome obstacles. Learn from the tenacity of Warren Buffett, whose unwavering faith in his investing methods helped him weather market turbulence and achieve unmatched success. Develop an unwavering feeling of self-assurance in your ability to recover from setbacks, remain composed in the face of difficulty, and project calmness.

3. Acquire a Determination-Focused Mindset

Resilience is fueled by determination, which keeps you going for your objectives even in the face of setbacks. Take inspiration from Elon Musk's tenacity as he persevered to transform the automobile and space sectors in spite of doubters. Develop a resolute, laser-focused mindset, establish specific goals, and never waver in your quest for achievement. Allow tenacity to be your beacon of hope throughout difficult times, inspiring you to succeed.

4. Accept Resilience as a Continuous Process

Being resilient is a constant process of development and adaptability rather than a final goal. Take a cue from Oprah Winfrey's tenacity, who overcome hardship to rise to prominence in the media, and adopt resilience as a continuous process of self-improvement and growth. Gain the ability to overcome obstacles, recover from failures, and grow stronger and more resilient with every experience. Accept resilience as a way of life and learn to navigate the ups and downs of obstacles with bravery and grace.

5. Learn the Technique of Stress Reduction for Resilience

Although stress will always be a part of the journey to success, developing resilience requires learning how to manage it. Take a cue from Bill Gates' approach, who places a high value on stress reduction and self-care in order to handle the demands of a fast-paced existence. Learn how to effectively manage stress by practicing self-care, mindfulness, and healthy coping strategies that help you feel and think more positively. Develop your resilience by learning how to properly manage stress and keep your equilibrium when faced with hardship.

6. Seek Advice and Mentorship to Develop Your Resilience

Building resilience and overcoming obstacles with grace and wisdom require mentorship and direction. Consider Richard Branson as an example, who looked to seasoned businessmen for guidance in navigating the erratic waters of the commercial world. Look for mentors who can motivate, advise, and share insightful knowledge with you in order to build your resilience and provide you the tools you need to overcome obstacles head-on. Accept mentoring as a tool to help you develop personally and strengthen your resilience while you work toward success.

7. Develop Your Growth and Self-Reflection to Master Resilience

A useful technique for developing resilience and personal development is self-reflection. Take a cue from Mark Zuckerberg, who leverages introspection to propel creativity and expansion at Facebook. Take stock of your talents and shortcomings, reflect on your life, and make a commitment to ongoing development. Adopt a growth attitude that is fueled by self-awareness, flexibility, and an unwavering quest for perfection. Use self-reflection to strengthen your inner strength and increase your resilience when faced with challenges.

Techniques for Retaining Clarity and Focus

Welcome to a life-changing adventure into the world of clarity and focus, two things that the richest and most accomplished people in the world admire for being crucial to their unmatched success. This chapter explores the fundamentals of staying focused and clear by drawing on the experiences and wisdom of notable individuals who have successfully used these techniques to improve their lives and achievements. Come along as we explore seven tactical approaches to developing steadfast focus and crystal-clear clarity that can catapult you into remarkable accomplishments.

1. Create a Vision That Spurs Your Enthusiasm

The foundation of clarity and focus, vision steers your course toward achievement with unyielding resolve. Create a captivating vision that sparks your enthusiasm and propels your journey by taking inspiration from Steve Jobs' visionary leadership, who revolutionized Apple with his audacious and inventive vision. Establish your mission, make big plans, and make sure everything you do is in line with a distinct vision that will help you navigate obstacles and divert your attention.

2. Establish Priorities with Unwavering Accuracy

Setting priorities is essential to keeping clarity and focus in the face of conflicting demands. Take a cue from Jeff Bezos, who at Amazon uses the obsession with the consumer as a guiding principle, and use merciless precision to set priorities that support your objectives. Set priorities, get rid of distractions, and focus your time and efforts on the things that will have the biggest influence and help you get closer to your goal.

3. Accept Mindfulness to Become Present-Moment Aware

By keeping you rooted in the present and promoting mental clarity, mindfulness is an effective technique for developing attention and clarity. To quiet the noise and distractions that prevent you from focusing, adopt present moment awareness. Oprah Winfrey is a great example of this, including mindfulness and meditation into her everyday routine. Engage in mindfulness practices to improve decision-making clarity and attention, such as deep breathing, visualization, and sensory awareness.

4. Learn the Art of Effective Time Management

Maintaining focus and clarity in the fast-paced world of success requires effective time management. Learn the art of time management to maximize productivity and attention, and take a cue from Warren Buffett, who is renowned for his methodical approach to time management and prioritizing of key work. Make use of time management techniques, to-do lists, and the Pomodoro method to plan your day, manage your time wisely, and stay laser-focused on reaching your objectives.

5. Develop a Growth Mentality to Be More Adaptable

Maintaining concentration and clarity in the face of obstacles and failures is facilitated by adopting a growth mentality. Grow a growth mindset that values learning and adaptation by taking a cue from Elon Musk's tenacity, who views setbacks as chances for improvement and creativity. Accept setbacks as chances for personal development, learn from your errors, and have an open mind to fresh viewpoints and ideas that will help you focus and see obstacles more clearly.

6. Seek Privacy to Gain Reflective Understanding

By creating a space for reflection and introspection, solitude can be a useful ally in preserving clarity and focus. Seek out times of calm isolation to clear your head and establish focus on your priorities and goals. Take a cue from Bill Gates, who appreciates this kind of time for introspection and strategic planning. To improve attention and clarity, make deliberate time for solitude—whether it is through silent retreats, nature walks, or everyday introspection.

———◆———

7. CREATE ROBUST SUPPORT and Accountability Networks

Maintaining concentration and clarity on your path to achievement requires creating robust networks of responsibility and support. Draw inspiration from Mark Zuckerberg's collaborative style, as he uses networks to get input and support for his business ventures. Establish relationships with peers, mentors, and accountability partners who will keep you accountable and promote your development. Embrace a network of people you can trust to inspire and push you to maintain accountability, focus, and alignment with your goals.

Part III

CONNECTIONS AND IMPACT

Chapter 5: Establishing Genuine Relationships

Chapter 6: The Craft of Persuasion

Chapter 5
Establishing Genuine Relationships

Welcome to a life-changing journey into the skill of creating genuine connections—a vital component that the most powerful and wealthy people in the world value for its enormous influence on both personal and professional success. This engaging section explores the fundamentals of developing real connections via personal stories and perspectives from forward-thinking leaders who have used the strength of true partnerships to improve their lives and achieve more success. Come along as we share seven smart strategies for developing real connections that will lead to unheard-of success.

1. Accept Vulnerability in Order to Be Authentic

Building true connections requires embracing vulnerability since it promotes sincere interactions and strengthens bonds. Take a cue from the bravery of Brené Brown, who is well-known for her research on authenticity and vulnerability, and embrace vulnerability as a strength that enables you to be who you truly are. Establish a foundation of trust and authenticity in your relationships by being transparent about your real stories, worries, and aspirations. This will allow others to connect with your true essence.

2. Engage in Empathetic Listening Practices to Foster Empathy

Authentic connections can be forged by active listening, which shows others that you genuinely care about them. Take inspiration from Bill Gates's sympathetic listening techniques, as he is well-known for his capacity to actively engage and comprehend a range of viewpoints. Engage in active listening yourself to foster stronger connections. To establish rapport and create real relationships based on respect and understanding, listen intently, try to understand others before you are understood, and give validation to what other people are saying and feeling.

<hr />

3. BE COMPASSIONATE and Encourage Real Relationships

Building real connections based on compassion, empathy, and reciprocal care requires both empathy and support. Take a cue from Warren Buffett, who is well-known for his compassionate leadership and encouragement of others' development and welfare, and provide compassion and support in your interpersonal interactions. Authentic ties based on empathy and solidarity can be fostered by demonstrating genuine caring, lending a helpful hand, and celebrating others' accomplishments.

4. Build Trust by Being Reliable and Consistent

Genuine connections are based on trust, which is based on consistency, dependability, and integrity in both your words and deeds. Develop trust through your behaviors by taking cues from Oprah Winfrey, who is renowned for her integrity and constant moral standards in all of her relationships and pursuits. Keep your word, be open with others, and maintain your moral principles to establish genuine relationships based on respect and dependability.

5. Honor Inclusivity and Diversity to Build Stronger Bonds

By accepting diverse viewpoints, experiences, and backgrounds, celebrating diversity and inclusivity strengthens your relationships. Celebrate diversity in your relationships and take inspiration from Tim Cook's inclusive leadership, who promotes diversity and inclusion at Apple. In order to create richer and more genuine connections that expand your ideas and experiences, interact with a varied variety of people, appreciate differences, and cultivate an inclusive environment that values and embraces diversity.

6. Give with generosity and sincerity

Since generosity shows kindness, real concern for others, and generosity of spirit, it is a significant factor in the development of authentic connections. Take inspiration from Mark Zuckerberg's humanitarian endeavors, as he dedicates his fortune to social influence and charity causes, and extend generosity in your relationships. By genuinely providing your time, resources, and support to people without expecting anything in return, you can build relationships built on appreciation, kindness, and sincere concern for others.

7. Seek Sincere Input for Development and Relationships

Seeking sincere feedback encourages constructive criticism, introspection, and interpersonal learning, all of which serve as catalysts for growth and deeper connections. Seek for honest opinions from others, using Jeff Bezos's approach of appreciating input as a tool for innovation and constant development at Amazon. In order to create genuine alliances based on learning and development from both parties, it is important to ask for and welcome honest and constructive criticism, listen to it with an open mind, and utilize it to improve self-awareness, growth, and connection in your relationships.

Developing Deeply Meaningful Bonds

1. Authenticity Is Essential for Sincere Connections

Meaningful relationships are built on authenticity, which goes beyond appearances and pretense to forge genuine bonds. Take a cue from Elon Musk's honesty, who is renowned for taking a direct and sincere approach to both success and failure, and be true to who you are in all of your relationships. Establish relationships based on respect, trust, and a sincere connection by being vulnerable, sharing your tales from the heart, and staying loyal to your principles.

2. Empathy: The Link Between Compassion and Understanding

Empathy is the link that binds brains and hearts together, promoting comprehension and strengthening emotional ties in interpersonal relationships. Cultivate empathy in your relationships by taking a hint from Warren Buffett, who values understanding and compassion in his dealings with people. To build deep connections based on compassion and understanding, listen with an open heart, make an effort to understand viewpoints that are different from your own, and extend kindness and support.

3. Gratitude: The Money of Relationships

Generosity is a strong energy that fosters reciprocity and gives partnerships a feeling of plenty. Consider Bill Gates, whose humanitarian endeavors have improved lives all across the world, and model generosity in all that you do. Donate kindly, generously, and without anticipating anything in return. This creates friendships based on mutual respect, gratitude, and a feeling of purpose.

4. Trust is the cornerstone of enduring relationships.

Meaningful relationships are based on trust, which includes being dependable, honest, and open in all of your dealings. Take a cue from

Jeff Bezos, who has demonstrated trustworthiness throughout his tenure at Amazon, and make developing trust a top priority in your interactions. To build relationships based on trust and long-lasting relationships, keep your word, talk honestly and openly, and act consistently.

5. Interaction: The Vital Sign of Relationship

Relationships need effective communication to be deeper in terms of emotional connection, dispute resolution, and promoting understanding. Develop your communication abilities for deep connections by taking inspiration from Oprah Winfrey, a master of genuine and powerful conversation. Make an effort to listen intently, communicate honestly and freely, and have meaningful conversations that help people connect and get along.

6. Respect: The Connection's Compass

Respect acknowledges each person's inherent worth and dignity and serves as a compass for interactions with others. Practice respect in your relationships by taking a cue from Tim Cook's treatment of diversity and inclusivity at Apple. Respect differences, express gratitude for the viewpoints and experiences of others, and cultivate an inclusive atmosphere that celebrates variety in order to build relationships based on acceptance and respect for one another.

7. Thinking Back: The Way to Growth and Self-Awareness

Reflection encourages reflection, learning, and self-improvement and serves as a catalyst for deeper connections and personal progress. Adopt Mark Zuckerberg's reflective approach, which emphasizes self-awareness and lifelong learning, and welcome introspection in your interpersonal interactions. Evaluate what you've done, get input from others, and utilize reflection as a technique for self-awareness, personal development, and improving relationships with others. This will help you build lasting bonds based on understanding and personal progress.

Both Active Listening and Effective Communication

Discover the seven fundamental strategies to learn successful communication and active listening based on the real-life experiences of the world's wealthiest people and visionary leaders. Step into the realm of the elite and unlock the secrets to transforming communication. Learn how to use communication to strengthen your connections, advance your career and personal success, and establish yourself as a leader in any industry. Prepare to master the art of successful communication and active listening to set yourself up for unmatched success by utilizing the knowledge of the top.

1. lucidity: The Influence Language

Clarity is the first step toward communicating effectively and is essential to delivering your message with impact and accuracy. Take a cue from Warren Buffett, who is well-known for having a direct and concise communication style that connects with people all over the world. To exert influence and leave a lasting impression, communicate simply, avoid using jargon, and make sure your message is understandable.

2. Empathy: The Vital Sign of a Relationship

Understanding others' ideas and feelings via empathy enables you to connect with them more deeply. Empathy is the foundation of meaningful communication. Draw inspiration from Bill Gates' compassionate demeanor, as he always demonstrates genuine concern and empathy when engaging with others. Active listening, acknowledging feelings, and empathetic behavior toward others are ways to develop rapport, establish trust, and fortify enduring connections.

3. Sincerity: The Key to Gaining Trust

Being genuine draws people in and builds a foundation of trust in communication. It works like a magnet. Consider Jeff Bezos' sincerity; he speaks with honesty and conviction in all of his encounters, winning the respect of both staff members and customers. To establish trust, credibility, and authenticity in your communication, stay true to who you are, speak from the heart, and line your words with your principles.

4. Respect: The Foundation for Cooperation

Collaborative communication is based on respect, which acknowledges the worth and viewpoints of others in every exchange. Take a cue from Tim Cook's treatment of diversity and inclusivity at Apple, which promotes an environment of mutual respect and cooperation. Respectful communication fosters mutual respect, tolerance for differing viewpoints, and the enhancement of teamwork, creativity, and innovation.

5. Commentary: The Source of Development

Feedback offers insightful opinions and useful insights to improve communication efficacy, which serves as a catalyst for both professional and personal growth. Take a cue from Elon Musk's communication style, which is characterized by constant development and openness to criticism. Get input from people, be open to helpful criticism, and use it as a tool to help you become a better communicator and learn how to work with a variety of audiences.

6. Flexibility: The Secret to Adaptability

To demonstrate your adaptability and versatility, you must be able to navigate the challenges of communicating with a variety of audiences and in a variety of settings. Take a note from Mark Zuckerberg, who skillfully adjusts his communication approach to connect with various audiences and stakeholders. To connect authentically and interact with a wide spectrum of people, be flexible, adjust your message to the situation, and prove your communication adaptability.

7. Being There: The Craft of Involvement

The art of being present involves giving someone your whole attention while paying attention, showing respect, and showing that you genuinely want to talk to them. Pay attention to Oprah Winfrey's captivating demeanor and keen listening abilities, since these capture crowds and foster meaningful connections. To demonstrate respect, establish trust, and forge deep connections through your presence and careful listening, engage in mindfulness practices, keep eye contact, and be totally present in all situations.

Chapter 6
The Craft Of Persuasion

Discover the techniques of the world's wealthiest people and visionary leaders in "The Art of Influence," and learn how to use your inner power with grace and mastery. Learn the essential tactics gleaned from actual experiences to improve your effect, influence people, and establish yourself as a force for change in any field. Prepare yourself for a life-changing experience that will help you realize your full potential and develop into a skilled communicator and leader.

1. Strategic Narrative: Engaging Emotions and Thoughts

Storytelling is the foundation of influence; visionaries such as Elon Musk utilize it to their advantage to capture audiences' attention. Write engrossing stories that move your audience, arouse feelings, and motivate action. Develop the ability to craft a well-planned narrative that will effectively, authentically, and purposefully communicate your message to the people you want to influence.

2. Charming Presence: Taking Charge and Getting Noticed

Leverage the captivating aura of eminent figures such as Richard Branson to effortlessly command attention and influence others. Develop a self-assured attitude, radiate charm, and create an alluring presence that makes people want to be around you. Utilize your inner self-assurance, uphold a powerful body language, and become an expert in nonverbal communication to project authority and influence in any circumstance.

3. Strategic Networking: Establishing Strong Links

Strategic networking is essential to influence, as Warren Buffett demonstrates by using his extensive network to inform important choices. Develop deep connections, get in touch with influential people in your field, and build a robust network that provides access to resources and opportunities. Make the most of networking opportunities, online resources, and people skills to broaden your network and establish enduring relationships that will accelerate your achievement.

4. Emotional Intelligence: Perceiving and Developing Other People

Jeff Bezos's ability to comprehend the demands and preferences of his customers is a perfect example of how empathy and emotional intelligence are essential elements of persuasion. Gain emotional intelligence by learning to recognize and comprehend other people's emotions and adjusting your communication style to suit their needs. Establishing trust and influence in your relationships requires you to listen intently, empower others by respecting their opinions and feelings, and act with real caring.

5. Strategic Persuasion: Handling Influence Power

Learn the art of persuasion from accomplished negotiators such as Bill Gates to successfully traverse the difficulties of influence. To influence opinions and influence decisions, hone your persuasive communication skills, make use of emotional and logical arguments, and present your ideas in an appealing way. To effectively accomplish your targeted goals, know what motivates and stimulates your audience, customize your persuasive strategies, and influence outcomes.

6. Adaptive Leadership: Using Flexibility and Influence to Lead

Tim Cook's adaptable leadership style at Apple demonstrates the need of adaptive leadership in effectively influencing others. Demonstrate flexibility in decision-making, adjust your leadership style to suit various contexts and people, and encourage teams to welcome change and creativity. Set a good example, communicate intelligibly and adaptably, and enable others to accomplish group objectives by exercising adaptive leadership that shapes favorable results.

7. Effective Communication: Using Precision to Amplify Your Message

Mark Zuckerberg's ability to engage multiple stakeholders through clear communication is an example of effective communication, which is the cornerstone of influence. Develop your communication abilities, deliver your message with accuracy and clarity, and craft your message such that it will appeal to the people you are speaking to. To make an effect and influence others with authenticity and authority, engage in impactful communication, ask insightful questions, and practice active listening.

Using Influence in an Ethical Way

G reetings from a trip that explores ethical persuasion and impact, going beyond simple influence. In this section, we present seven successful tactics that show how to wield influence in an ethical, spiritual, and effective way, taking inspiration from the wealthiest people on the planet and visionary leaders.

---

1. GENUINENESS ABOVE All: Setting a good example

Authenticity is the cornerstone of ethical influence, and it is a quality that influential people like Warren Buffett and Oprah Winfrey promote. Set a good example, uphold your moral principles, and be genuine in all of your interactions. When your behavior is consistent with your convictions, you build credibility and trust, which lays the groundwork for ethical influence that has a deep impact on other people.

2. Accountability and Transparency: Developing Openness to Foster Trust

The actions of Satya Nadella and Elon Musk serve as excellent examples of how accountability and transparency are the cornerstones of ethical influence. Accept accountability for your actions, communicate honestly, and exchange information freely. Establishing a culture of transparency and responsibility helps you gain the audience's trust and tell a powerful story of integrity that creates the conditions for ethical influence to grow.

3. Empowerment via Empathy: Seeing and Developing Other People

The sympathetic leadership of Sheryl Sandberg and Tim Cook serves as evidence that empathy is a potent instrument for ethical influence. Develop empathy for other people, make an effort to comprehend their viewpoints, and provide them the tools they need to realize their full potential. You create strong bonds by acting with empathy, compassion, and understanding, which opens the door for moral influence to encourage constructive change and development.

4. Cooperative Decision-Making: Promoting Diversity and Inclusivity

As demonstrated by Jeff Bezos and Indra Nooyi's inclusive policies, collaboration is essential to ethical influence in order to drive impact and innovation. Encourage a collaborative culture, accept a range of viewpoints, and participate in inclusive decision-making procedures. Respecting the opinions of all parties involved helps to strengthen the voices of others, create a sense of community, and build a cooperative atmosphere that supports moral impact and group achievement.

5. Leadership with a Purpose: Motivating for a Greater Good

Leaders such as Marc Benioff and Mary Barra epitomize ethical impact through their purpose-driven leadership. Establish a distinct goal that transcends financial gain, motivate people with a greater purpose, and unite them behind a common goal. By setting an example of purposeful leadership, you inspire others to be passionate, driven, and dedicated. This sense of purpose propels ethical influence in the direction of significant and lasting results.

6. Honesty in Practice: Acting Out What You Talk About

In terms of ethical impact, integrity is unassailable, as demonstrated by the steadfast integrity of Susan Wojcicki and Bill Gates. Keep oneself accountable to moral standards, act with honesty, and uphold high ethical standards. You gain credibility, respect, and a reputation for moral leadership that inspires confidence when you continuously practice what you preach.

7. Ongoing Education and Development: Changing Ethical Impact

Growth in the field of ethical influence is an ongoing process of development and adaptation, as leaders like Ginni Rometty and Jeff Weiner have embraced. Make a commitment to lifelong learning, ask for feedback, and welcome both professional and personal development. You may hone your ethical influence, broaden your impact, and encourage others to follow in your footsteps as you pursue excellence and ethical leadership by remaining agile, adaptable, and receptive to fresh viewpoints.

Motivating Others With Your Deeds

1. Setting a Good Example: The Influence of Sincerity

A key component of motivating people through action is setting an example, which is something that successful people like Bill Gates and Warren Buffett do well. Genuineness develops credibility and trust, and it provides direction for people looking for inspiration. By exhibiting honesty, openness, and unwavering devotion to your principles, you provide a powerful example that inspires others to adopt moral leadership.

2. Impactful Philanthropy: Contributing to a Greater Good

The philanthropic pursuits of individuals such as Jeff Bezos and Mark Zuckerberg demonstrate the effectiveness of philanthropy as a means of motivating others to take action. Giving back to the community, endorsing deserving causes, and actively tackling social issues are ways to show that you are dedicated to bringing about positive change and cultivating a culture of compassion and giving. Others are motivated to give to worthwhile causes and change the world by your charitable deeds.

3. Innovative Leadership: Using Innovation to Drive Change

As seen by the inspirational leadership of Elon Musk and Larry Page, innovation is a major force behind inspiration translated into action. You motivate others to think creatively, accept change, and pursue greatness by seeking out novel ideas, upending established beliefs, and stretching the bounds of what is feasible. Those around you become curious, ambitious, and driven to keep getting better as a result of your creative efforts.

4. Empowering Others: Fostering Development and Growth

As enabling leaders like Sheryl Sandberg and Tim Cook have shown, empowering others is a potent method to motivate through action. People may reach their goals and reach their full potential when you invest in their team's development, create a culture of mentorship, and offer growth chances. Your dedication to enabling others gives them self-assurance, resiliency, and a feeling of direction, motivating them to succeed and make significant contributions to common objectives.

5. Sustainable Practices: Environmental Responsibility at the Center

Advocates for sustainability such as Indra Nooyi and Richard Branson have demonstrated that taking environmental responsibility is a powerful means of inspiring action. You may show that you are committed to protecting the environment for future generations by supporting eco-friendly programs, decreasing your influence on the environment, and advocating for sustainable practices. Your environmentally friendly deeds encourage others to follow suit, encourage sustainability in their own lives, and help create a more sustainable and greener future.

6. Inclusivity and Diversity: Promoting Equity and Compassion

It is a transforming strategy to inspire via action to promote diversity and inclusivity, as inclusive leaders like Satya Nadella and Mary Barra have embraced. You can encourage others to accept diversity, respect inclusivity, and give empathy first priority in their interactions by advocating for diversity, supporting inclusivity, and cultivating an environment of equality and empathy. Your dedication to diversity and inclusivity encourages people to appreciate differences and create a more inclusive society by fostering a sense of acceptance, respect, and understanding.

7.Embracing growth and agility through ongoing learning and adaptation

Leaders that are adaptive, like Jack Ma and Angela Merkel, inspire people via action by embracing constant learning and change. You encourage a culture of development, resiliency, and innovation by placing a high value on learning, looking for new challenges, and adjusting to changing conditions. Your dedication to constant development and adjustment inspires others to welcome change, exercise critical thought, and shift with the times, fostering an inventive and nimble spirit in all that you do.

Part IV
Vitality and Health
Chapter 7 : Wholesome Health
Chapter 8: Energy Administration

Chapter 7
Wholesome Health

Greetings from a transformative journey that explores the comprehensive nature of human existence and leads to optimal well-being and true richness beyond material possessions. This chapter delves into seven fundamental methods for fostering holistic well-being, all derived from the experiences of the wealthiest people on the planet, visionary leaders, and kind influencers. You will be able to access the boundless benefits of robust health, lasting happiness, and inner peace by adopting these techniques and aligning with the principles of holistic wellness. This will pave the way for an unmatched life of success and joy.

1. Mindful Presence: Fostering Inner Calm Despite Achievement

In today's fast-paced world of prosperity and achievement, mindfulness emerges as the primary component of overall wellbeing. Prominent figures such as Oprah Winfrey and Warren Buffett serve as prime examples of how mindful presence may promote mental clarity and inner serenity amidst the pressures of a high-achieving existence. You can create the foundation for a harmonious living that transcends material accomplishments and resonates with true richness from within by engaging in mindfulness practices, developing awareness of the present moment, and tending to your quiet mind.

2. Physical Vitality: Caring for the Body's Temple

People who value their health and fitness, such as Serena Williams and Richard Branson, demonstrate how important physical vitality is to holistic well-being. You honor the temple of your body and create the groundwork for bright health and long-lasting energy by making regular exercise a priority, feeding your body with good foods, and giving rest and rejuvenation top priority. Physical vitality not only makes you more resilient and productive, but it also gives your life energy in all its forms.

3. Emotional Intelligence: Using Emotions to Our Advantage

Holistic well-being is a result of emotional intelligence, as exemplified by leaders who face obstacles head-on and come out on top—people like Sheryl Sandberg and Jeff Bezos. By cultivating healthy relationships, regulating stress, and increasing self-awareness, you may harness the power of emotions to create emotional balance and meaningful connections. Being emotionally intelligent makes it possible for you to handle life's ups and downs with sincerity, empathy, and composure, which improves your overall wellbeing and creates a peaceful interior environment.

4. Spiritual Link: Discovering Significance and Intent

The spiritual practices of individuals such as Bill Gates and the Dalai Lama attest to the profound well-being and fulfillment that may be derived from a strong spiritual connection. You can access a source of spiritual richness that surpasses worldly wealth by investigating your beliefs, making a connection with a higher purpose, and cultivating a feeling of significance that goes beyond material pursuits. Having a spiritual connection gives you direction, a sense of purpose, and interconnectedness that raises your wellbeing to new heights.

5. Social Support: Fostering Soul-Nourishing Relationships

Compassionate leaders who value community and collaboration, such as Melinda Gates and Mark Zuckerberg, recognize the importance of social support for holistic well-being. You can build a network of support that helps you get through the ups and downs of life by cultivating empathy, helping others in their progress, and promoting their well-being. Social ties strengthen your well-being and deepen your experience of true riches by giving you a sense of joy, belonging, and resilience.

6. Financial Well-Being: Matching Resources with Principles

As ethical leaders like Elon Musk and Feike Sijbesma have emphasized, financial wellness is not just about accumulating wealth but also about matching your financial resources with your ideals and overall well-being. You may develop a sense of wealth that transcends tangible belongings by practicing generosity and stewardship, investing in causes that align with your beliefs, and managing your money sensibly. Being financially well-adjusted enables you to make deliberate decisions that promote your welfare, further the common good, and cultivate a feeling of abundance that arises from being in harmony with your core beliefs.

7. Integrating Work and Life: Juggling Achievement and Self-Care

Empirical evidence of the importance of work-life integration for overall well-being comes from executives who support work-life balance and self-care, such as Satya Nadella and Tim Cook. You establish a rhythm that is harmonious and nourishes every part of your existence when you prioritize professional accomplishment with time set aside for rest, relaxation, and personal fulfillment. Work-life integration enables you to achieve professional success while preserving a sense of balance, contentment, and inner harmony that upholds your wellbeing and provides holistic wealth to your life.

Juggling One's Mental, Emotional, And Physical Well-Being

1.Give Physical Vitality First Priority

Follow the lead of prosperous businessmen such as Jeff Bezos and Richard Branson, who recognize the need of physical health in maintaining their high-energy lifestyles. To maximize your physical well-being, make regular exercise an indispensible part of your routine, feed your body wholesome meals that energize and nourish it, and make sure you get enough sleep and recuperation. Making physical vitality a priority helps you build a solid foundation for resilience and general health, which will allow you to flourish in all facets of your life.

2. Develop Mental Health

Emulate the success of forward-thinking individuals like Elon Musk and Bill Gates, who place a high value on mental health. Take part in mentally stimulating activities, including reading, picking up new skills, or meditating and being mindful. Develop a growth mentality, be resilient in the face of adversity, and look for solutions that advance your intellectual wellbeing. By practicing mental fitness, you can improve your creativity, sharpen your mind, and develop the mental toughness required to deal with the challenges of today's hectic environment.

---

3. ACKNOWLEDGE YOUR emotional intelligence

Take inspiration from compassionate role models such as Melinda Gates and Oprah Winfrey, who demonstrate the efficacy of emotional intelligence in cultivating significant connections and individual development. Gain self-awareness, learn how to effectively control your emotions, and work on your empathy for other people. You can build genuine connections, manage stress with grace, and negotiate interpersonal dynamics with compassion when you embrace emotional intelligence. Building resilience, creating harmony in relationships, and taking care of your emotional wellbeing all depend on having high emotional intelligence.

4. Foster a Spiritual Bond

Be inspired by spiritual masters who stress the value of fostering a spiritual connection for overall well-being, such as the Dalai Lama and Deepak Chopra. Examine your ideas, establish a connection with a greater purpose, and partake in activities that enhance your spiritual fulfillment. Developing a spiritual connection allows you to access a reservoir of inner knowledge, tranquility, and fortitude that surpasses financial prosperity. A sense of meaning, purpose, and connection that comes from spiritual sustenance enhances life and gives you the ability to face obstacles head-on with poise and clarity.

5. Establish a Community of Support

Take a cue from well-known philanthropists like Warren Buffett and Mark Zuckerberg, who recognize the need of creating a community that is helpful for both individual and group well-being. Develop connections that encourage and uplift you, surround yourself with uplifting people, and lend a helping hand to those in need. You may build a network of allies who will celebrate your accomplishments, strengthen your resilience, and offer emotional support by cultivating a supportive community. Sustaining mental and emotional well-being, creating a feeling of community, and improving general well-being all depend on having a robust support network.

6. Connect Money and Well-Being

Seek for moral role models such as Tim Cook and Feike Sijbesma, who place a high value on financial security as a way to promote social influence and overall wellness. Be fiscally responsible, make investments in causes that share your values, and engage in acts of stewardship and charity. You can cultivate an abundance that transcends material wealth by coordinating your financial resources with your aspirations for your well-being. Being financially well-adjusted enables you to make deliberate decisions that promote your general well-being, further the common good, and heighten your feelings of wealth and fulfillment.

7. Aim for Equilibrium Work-Life

Take up the philosophy of prosperous businessmen such as Satya Nadella and Sheryl Sandberg, who see work-life balance as essential to long-term success and well-being. Establish boundaries to safeguard your wellbeing, give self-care and relaxation first priority, and work toward striking a balance between your personal and professional obligations. Achieving work-life balance enables you to lead a sustainable lifestyle that uplifts your whole self, increases your output, and spreads happiness and contentment. Maintaining overall wellbeing, avoiding burnout, and promoting a sense of holistic riches all depend on striking a balance between work and personal life.

Exercise, Diet, and Stress Reduction

L earn how to synchronize your mental, emotional, and physical health with the practices of high achievers.

1. Boost Your Achievement with Diet

Take a cue from affluent businessmen such as Elon Musk and Mark Zuckerberg, who regard good nutrition as essential to their high-achieving lifestyles. Make the most of your diet by including foods high in nutrients that will fuel your mind and body, improving your energy and cognitive abilities. Adopt a well-rounded eating strategy that enhances your general health and encourages vigor and longevity. You build the groundwork for optimum health, mental clarity, and sustained performance in all facets of your life when you use nutrition to drive your achievement.

2. Improve Your Results with Exercise

Follow the fitness routines of successful businesspeople and athletes like Serena Williams and Jeff Bezos, who recognize the positive effects of exercise on the body and mind. Include regular exercise in your regimen to improve your general health and well-being by increasing your energy, strength, and endurance. Take part in stimulating and demanding activities that stretch your boundaries and help you reach your full potential. By improving your performance via exercise, you develop self-control, perseverance, and a solid physical base that enable you to overcome obstacles and succeed in all that you do.

3. Learn Stress Reduction to Perform at Your Best

Learn from the success of resilience gurus like Bill Gates and Oprah Winfrey, who have mastered the art of stress management and can perform well under pressure. Learn effective coping strategies to handle stress and hardship, such as deep breathing techniques, mindfulness, and meditation. Make self-care and relaxation a priority to revitalize your body and mind and maintain equilibrium and serenity despite the pressures of daily life. You can improve your capacity to remain focused, make wise decisions, and perform at your best in trying conditions by becoming an expert in stress management.

4. Develop Mental Quickness to Achieve Success

Take a cue from forward-thinking individuals such as Tim Cook and Warren Buffett, who value mental acuity as a crucial tool for negotiating intricate corporate environments. Engage your mind with creative endeavors, problem-solving exercises, and ongoing education to broaden your mental horizons and enhance cognitive performance. Encourage a growth attitude that can handle uncertainty, accept change, and adjust to new difficulties. By practicing mental agility, you can improve your cognitive function, encourage creativity, and build the resilience you need to face obstacles head-on and seize new chances.

---

5. ADOPT EMOTIONAL Intelligence as a Basis for Genuine Leadership

Take a cue from compassionate leaders such as Melinda Gates and Richard Branson, who recognize the value of emotional intelligence in developing genuine relationships and establishing trust. Develop self-awareness, empathy, and emotional control to handle social situations with tact, understanding, and empathy. To create enduring connections based on cooperation and trust, hone your communication skills and use active listening strategies. Adopting an emotional intelligence mindset improves your ability to empathize, connect, and lead effectively. It also leaves a positive impression on others and promotes an environment of mutual respect and support.

---

6. PROMOTE EMOTIONAL health and inner serenity

Seek guidance from spiritual masters who stress the significance of fostering inner peace and emotional well-being for holistic wellbeing, such as the Dalai Lama and Deepak Chopra. To cultivate calm and harmony within, practice techniques that support emotional balance, such as journaling, meditation, or gratitude exercises. To develop a sense of purpose and fulfillment, connect with your inner self and stay true to your values and convictions. You can develop resilience, self-compassion, and a profound feeling of inner harmony that enables you to face obstacles with grace, kindness, and honesty by fostering inner peace and emotional well-being.

7. Leverage Rich Wellness Integration's Power

Integrate mental acuity, emotional intelligence, physical activity, stress reduction, and nutrition into a well-rounded framework for prosperous health integration. Adopt a holistic perspective on health that balances the mind, body, and spirit to promote inner peace, prosperity, and optimal health. To reach your greatest potential and succeed in all facets of your life, establish a harmonious relationship between your physical, mental, and emotional well-being routines. Through the application of affluent wellness integration, you can improve your general state of health, develop resilience, and set out on a path to prosperity, abundance, and holistic wealth.

Chapter 8
Energy Administration

G reetings from a revolutionary journey that uses the art of energy management to achieve peak performance, success, and ultimate vitality. This chapter reveals the seven vital tactics that the wealthiest people on the planet and forward-thinking business executives use to maximize your energy and achieve unmatched achievement. "Energize Your Success" will enable you to realize your full potential, boost productivity, and create an abundant life by drawing on personal experiences and useful insights. Prepare to transform the way you handle energy and take yourself to previously unheard-of heights of success and satisfaction.

1. Customs of Reconstruction

Observe successful people such as Oprah Winfrey and Richard Branson, who place a high value on restorative routines as a means of recharging their batteries and continuing to operate at their best. To revitalize your mind, body, and soul, incorporate regular routines such as mindfulness, meditation, and nature walks. By setting aside time for self-care and renewal, you cultivate a steady supply of energy that powers your achievement and improve your capacity to remain resilient, creative, and focused in the face of adversity.

2. Blocking out time strategically

Take a cue from successful time managers like Jeff Bezos and Elon Musk, who use deliberate time blocking to maximize output and save energy for important tasks. Set up certain time slots for concentrated work, artistic endeavors, and personal priorities. This can help you avoid becoming sidetracked or hopping between tasks, which can deplete your energy. By planning your day with intention and purpose, you maximize your efficiency and effectiveness in reaching your goals by making time for deep work, creative thinking, and strategic planning.

3. Movement with Awareness and Physical Energy

Accept the dedication to physical vitality exhibited by Mark Zuckerberg and Serena Williams, who place a high value on exercise and mindful movement to maintain their energy levels and improve their general wellbeing. Exercises that stimulate and enliven your body, like yoga, strength training, or outdoor sports, will increase your physical energy and mental clarity. Regular exercise helps you build a solid foundation of resilience and health that gives you the strength and drive to face obstacles head-on.

---

4. DIET FOR RENEWABLE Energy

Take a cue from Tim Cook and Warren Buffett, who recognize the critical role that diet plays in maintaining energy levels and encouraging peak performance. Nutrient-dense foods provide your body with the nourishment and fuel it needs to maintain mental clarity, physical stamina, and emotional stability. Embrace a mindful eating style, healthy foods, and water as the foundation of a balanced diet to maximize your nutrition and maintain your energy and vigor all day.

5. Mental acuity and emotional toughness

Use the mental acuity and emotional fortitude shown by Bill and Melinda Gates, who overcome obstacles with grace and flexibility by using their emotional intelligence and cognitive flexibility. Develop self-awareness, emotional control, and problem-solving abilities to handle stress, deal with uncertainty, and stay focused in the face of distractions. Gaining mental and emotional agility strengthens your inner resources, improves your ability to make decisions, and helps you establish a growth-oriented, resilient mentality that will lead you to success.

6. Positive Energy and Mindset Mastery

Take up the proactive, upbeat attitude that drives the success of visionary leaders like Sheryl Sandberg and Richard Branson, and embody their positive energy and mastery of mindset. Develop a growth mentality that views obstacles as chances for personal development, education, and creativity. This will help you stay motivated and move closer to your objectives. To cultivate a mindset of abundance, opportunity, and resilience, engage in gratitude practices, visualization exercises, and affirmation practices. This will infuse your undertakings with passion, purpose, and steadfast positivity.

7. Balancing Life and Work Energies

As successful businesspeople like Jeff Bezos and Tim Cook have shown, strive for harmony and balance in balancing work and life energies. These individuals place a high priority on work-life integration in order to maintain their vitality and wellbeing. Establish limits, assign responsibilities, and give self-care first priority to build a balanced life that balances work and play and fuels your happiness. Your life and work energies can be brought into harmony with intention and attention, establishing a steady rhythm that promotes wellbeing, creativity, and productivity in all facets of your life.

Maintaining Elevated Mood for Optimal Outcomes

Set off on a life-changing adventure towards unmatched achievement and optimal functioning as we explore the skill of maintaining elevated levels of energy. Inspired by the wealthiest people on the planet and by forward-thinking leaders, this chapter reveals seven tried-and-true methods to maximize your energy reserves, boost output, and catapult you into amazing success. This section aims to transform your energy management strategy and put you on the way to unmatched achievement and fulfillment through real-life experiences and useful ideas. Prepare to achieve peak performance by realizing your full potential, improving your performance, and starting a revolution.

1. Customs of Fortitude

See inside the lives of iconic figures like Oprah Winfrey and Richard Branson, who place a great value on resilience rituals to sustain their high levels of vitality and excellence. Incorporate self-care, mindfulness, and meditation into your daily routine to refuel and build resilience in the face of adversity. You may improve your concentration, creativity, and endurance by creating a sacred space for recovery. This opens the door to long-term success and wellbeing.

2. Deliberate Allocation of Energy

Learn from the energy allocation tactics of successful businessmen like Jeff Bezos and Elon Musk, who use efficiency and strategic planning to maximize their energy for high-impact endeavors. Setting priorities and focusing your attention on goals-aligned tasks helps you maintain physical and mental health for optimal performance. Accept deliberate energy management to reach your full potential and operate at your best with purpose and accuracy.

3. Revitalizing Exercise and Physical Well-Being

Take inspiration from Serena Williams and Mark Zuckerberg's dedication to physical vitality. They both place a high value on movement and exercise as a way to maintain their energy levels and advance general wellbeing. Take part in energetic exercises such as yoga, weight training, or outdoor sports to increase your physical and mental energy. Regular exercise strengthens your body's energy reserves, increasing your resilience and ability to perform at your best.

4. Diet for Renewable Energy

Adhere to the dietary guidance of Tim Cook and Warren Buffett, who are aware of the life-changing potential of healthy meals for maintaining energy levels and enhancing performance. Fill your body with nutrient-dense foods that promote emotional stability, physical stamina, and cerebral clarity. Embrace a well-rounded dietary strategy that places an emphasis on nutritious foods and fluids to energize your body and mind for long-term success and vitality.

———◉———

5. MENTAL TOUGHNESS and emotional intelligence

Take in the mental toughness and emotional intelligence of Bill and Melinda Gates, two people who overcome obstacles with grace and resiliency. Develop self-awareness, emotional control, and flexibility to handle stress and stay focused in the face of ambiguity. Gaining mental and emotional agility and intelligence for sustained peak performance helps you make better decisions, fortify your inner reserves, and establish a resilient attitude.

6. Positive Energy and Mindset Mastery

Be a living example of the positive energy and mindset mastery that Sheryl Sandberg and Richard Branson, two successful executives who foster optimism and proactive thinking, have advocated. Adopt a growth mindset that sees obstacles as chances for development, innovation, and change. To cultivate a positive mindset that drives you toward your goals with unrelenting passion and positivity, practice gratitude, visualization, and affirmations.

7. Balancing Work and Life Energy

As exemplified by Jeff Bezos and Tim Cook, who combine work and life goals for sustained vitality and well-being, strive for harmony in balancing work and life energies. Establish limits, give yourself first priority, assign responsibilities, and combine work and play in a way that balances both and gives you a sense of fulfillment and vitality. Productivity, creativity, and general well-being are all improved when you create a sustainable rhythm by balancing and intentionally directing the energies of your work and life.

Making Self-Care a Priority

1. Conscious Behavior
   See how Warren Buffett practices mindfulness to foster mental clarity and inner serenity in his day-to-day activities. Participating in mindful activities like writing, breathing exercises, or meditation helps you develop emotional resilience and a sense of present. Use mindfulness to lower stress, improve focus, and develop a positive outlook that will propel your quest for money and success.

2. Physical Activation
Learn from Elon Musk's example, who places a high value on maintaining physical vigor through regular movement and exercise. Physical exercise such as running, yoga, or strength training improves your brain clarity and creativity in addition to your physical health. Make an investment in your health by placing a high value on physical vitality. You'll notice an increase in energy and the ability to face obstacles head-on.

3. Food as Fuel
Take a cue from Tim Cook, who is aware of the life-changing potential of healthy foods in maintaining energy levels and enhancing performance. Consume nutrient-dense foods to fuel your body and promote general health and energy. Giving your body the fuel it needs to thrive—a balanced diet full of healthy foods and plenty of water—will increase your productivity and ability to accumulate riches.

4. Rest and Healing
Take a cue from Jeff Bezos about how to rest and recuperate. He understands the value of taking time off for creativity and renewal. Make relaxation, good sleep, and enough rest your top priorities to

avoid burnout and replenish your vitality. You may refuel your physical and mental reserves and create the conditions for long-term success and wealth development by respecting your desire for relaxation and downtime.

5. Mental Health

Examine Oprah Winfrey's methods for emotional well-being, as she places a strong emphasis on the value of emotional self-care and self-awareness. Develop emotional intelligence, self-compassion, and resilience to face obstacles head-on and with poise. Making emotional health a priority improves your relationships, judgment, and general sense of well-being, which opens the door to a prosperous and abundant life.

———◉———

6. LIMITATIONS AND Equilibrium

Take a cue from Bill Gates, who knows how important it is to create boundaries in order to safeguard his time and well-being. Set limits both personally and professionally, assign responsibilities, and develop the ability to decline engagements that sap your vitality. Maintaining a healthy work-life balance allows you to save up your energy for things that will help you reach your objectives, which will boost your output and success.

7. Self-Evaluation and Development

Accept self-evaluation and ongoing development, drawing inspiration from Mark Zuckerberg's growth attitude. Evaluate your progress on a regular basis, acknowledge your successes, and view setbacks as chances for improvement. By making a commitment to your own growth and development, you broaden your perspectives, increase your abilities, and get closer to success and prosperity.

Part V

Luxury and plenty

Chapter 9: managing your money

Chapter 10: mindset of abundance

Chapter 9
Mastery of Finance

S et off on a life-changing path to financial mastery as we explore the tactics used by the richest people on the planet to attain unmatched achievement. This chapter offers seven tried-and-true strategies for improving your financial well-being, all based on the experiences and wisdom of visionary leaders. "Financial Mastering" is a guide to achieving financial wealth and freedom, not just a chapter in a book. This chapter claims to transform your relationship with money and provide you the tools you need to leave a successful and prosperous legacy through creative problem-solving and practical knowledge.

1. Investing Strategically

Warren Buffett, who famously stated, "Rule No. 1: Never lose money. Rule No. 2: Never forget rule No. 1," is a wise investment advisor. Develop your skills in strategic investing by diversifying your holdings, doing in-depth research, and keeping up with current market conditions. You can gradually accumulate money and reduce risk on your path to financial mastery by adhering to a disciplined investing strategy and looking for long-term growth prospects.

---

2. MONETARY EDUCATION

Adopt the lifelong learning mentality that Bill Gates has espoused. He credits his success to his insatiable curiosity. Continue your education on investing methods, asset management, and personal finance. To increase your financial literacy and make wise decisions that get you closer to financial mastery, take workshops, read books, and consult with financial consultants.

3. Financial Self-Control and Budgeting

Adhere to Elon Musk's budgeting guidelines, which place a strong emphasis on financial accountability and restrained spending. Make a thorough budget that fits your financial objectives, keep a close eye on your spending, and live frugally every day. You can maximize your assets, optimize your savings, and quicken your journey to financial independence by becoming an expert budgeter and practicing sound financial management.

4. A mindset of entrepreneurship

Channel the enterprising spirit of Jeff Bezos, whose unwavering focus on innovation and customer-centricity revolutionized e-commerce. Develop an entrepreneurial mindset by looking for chances to improve, being willing to take calculated risks, and viewing failure as a necessary step on the path to success. You can find new business opportunities, generate various revenue streams, and open the door for exponential wealth development by embracing an entrepreneurial attitude.

5. Managing Debt Strategically

Take a cue from Oprah Winfrey's debt management tactics. She overcome hardship to create an empire by making wise financial choices. When investing in income-generating projects or acquiring assets, for example, use debt as a tool for strategic leverage. To improve your financial situation and attain long-term prosperity, prioritize paying off debt, stay away from high-interest loans, and keep a healthy balance between debt and assets.

6. Generosity and Charities

Follow in the philanthropic footsteps of Mark Zuckerberg, who places a high value on contributing to society and promoting good change through philanthropic projects. Develop a giving mindset by supporting organizations that change the world, giving to issues you care about, and offering your time. By engaging in acts of giving and philanthropy, you improve society and your financial path while also drawing prosperity and goodwill into your life.

7.Preservation of Wealth and Legacy Planning

Imagine a long-lasting legacy motivated by Tim Cook's wealth preservation tactics, which place a high priority on estate preparation and legacy planning for future generations. Create a thorough wealth preservation plan that combines trusts, estate planning, and wise asset allocation to protect your wealth and guarantee your heirs' access to it. You may make a lasting impression, ensure your family's future, and leave a financial legacy that lasts after your death by putting a strong emphasis on legacy planning and wealth preservation.

Developing Wealth by Making Wise Financial Choices

E nter a world where real-world success and financial expertise collide with "Wealth Creation Unleashed." Using the experiences of the richest people in the planet as our model, we reveal the methods for building wealth through wise financial choices. Prepare yourself for a life-changing experience as we provide seven effective tactics that will raise your level of money production and help you achieve financial prosperity. This book is the key to opening the door to financial prosperity and taking control of your financial future since it offers both practical insights and visionary wisdom.

1. Mastery of Strategic Investment

Learn the art of strategic investing directly from the Oracle of Omaha himself, Warren Buffett. Develop a long-term growth attitude, do thorough study, and become an expert in navigating the financial markets. Through astute investment choices, embrace diversification, remain up to date on market developments, and capitalize on compound interest to accelerate your wealth accumulation path.

2. Enhancement of Financial Education

Learn from Bill Gates's example and dedicate your life to expanding your understanding in personal finance. Explore the depths of investing techniques, wealth management, and financial literacy. Give yourself the knowledge and resources necessary to make wise choices that provide the framework for long-term wealth development. Never stop learning, whether it's through seminars, books, or professional advice, and you'll see your financial savvy reach new heights.

3. Financial Discipline and Brilliant Budgeting:

Take up Elon Musk's philosophy of frugal spending and learn how to budget and be financially responsible. Create a thorough budget that fits your financial objectives, keep a close eye on your spending, and develop frugal spending habits. Effective budgeting and a commitment to sound financial management set the stage for maximum savings, stable investments, and quick progress toward financial independence.

4. Empowerment of the Entrepreneurial Mindset:

Adopt Jeff Bezos's entrepreneurial attitude as you develop an innovative and growth-oriented mindset. Recognize possibilities, take measured chances, and consider failures stepping stones toward achievement. You can create exponential wealth development, various revenue sources, and creative initiatives by cultivating an entrepreneurial attitude. Seize the opportunity, think creatively, and watch as your quest to create money takes off.

5. Using Debt Strategically:

Apply Oprah Winfrey's calculated approach to debt management to your own situation and use debt as a means of accumulating wealth. Use debt wisely to finance growth projects, buy assets that will appreciate in value, and take advantage of investment opportunities. Make paying off debt your top priority, avoid taking out high-interest loans, and maintain a careful balance between debt and assets to best position yourself financially for long-term wealth building.

6. Generosity and Significant Giving:

Follow in Mark Zuckerberg's charitable footsteps and use giving to change the world in a meaningful way. Contribute to causes that are important to you, offer your time as a volunteer, and back programs that encourage good change. You can bring prosperity and kindness into your financial journey in addition to improving the lives of others by engaging in acts of charity and meaningful philanthropy.

7. Establishing Legacies and Preserving Wealth:

Consider leaving a legacy that will last for many years by following Tim Cook's lead in legacy planning and asset preservation. Create a thorough wealth preservation plan that incorporates trusts, estate planning, and wise asset allocation. Preserve your wealth, ensure the future of your family, and provide the foundation for a long-lasting financial legacy that you can leave behind after your death.

Making Smart Investments And Generating Passive Income

Start a life-changing journey towards financial abundance and long-term prosperity with "Passive Wealth Mastery." In this section, we explore the art of producing passive income and making sensible investments by learning from the wealthiest people on the planet. Discover seven effective techniques that will enable you to create passive income streams, navigate the complicated world of investments, and ensure a secure financial future. This book is your guide to learning the techniques of mastering wealth creation and achieving financial freedom. It includes real-life success stories and practical ideas.

1. Perspectives on Strategic Investing

Adopt the practice of strategic investing and gain insight into Warren Buffett's wealth management expertise. To build a diverse investing portfolio, delve deeply into the worlds of stocks, bonds, real estate, and other assets. To optimize your returns, carry out in-depth research, examine market patterns, and have a long-term outlook. Making wise investing choices grounded in solid principles opens the door to long-term wealth accumulation and monetary stability.

2. Generating Passive Income

Examine the world of passive income sources and learn from Robert Kiyosaki's approach. Accept the power of affiliate marketing, dividend-paying equities, rental properties, and royalties to produce steady cash flow with no work. You can develop financial resilience and unleash the potential for wealth creation without being restricted to a regular 9–5 work by developing various streams of passive income.

Allow your finances to work for you, and over time, observe as your passive income increases dramatically.

3. Mastery of Real Estate:

Emulate real estate tycoons such as Donald Trump and harness the potential of real estate investments to amass fortune. Learn how to spot cheap assets with significant growth potential and explore options in residential, commercial, and rental properties. Utilize the advantages of property appreciation, rental income, and tax savings to build a profitable real estate portfolio that forms the basis of your passive income plan. You can create the groundwork for long-term wealth building and financial security by making wise real estate investments.

4. Excellence in Dividend Investing:

Create a passive income-generating portfolio of dividend-paying stocks by following Warren Buffett's dividend investing technique. Pay attention to businesses that have a track record of reliable dividend increases, solid financial results, and long-term business strategies. Reinvest dividends to take advantage of compound interest and quicken the accumulation of your wealth. Accepting dividend investing helps you establish a steady stream of passive income that is resilient to market swings and yields long-term gains.

5. Empowerment of Online Businesses:

To generate passive income streams, take a cue from Jeff Bezos and take use of the enormous opportunities presented by the digital economy. Examine opportunities for passive revenue generation such as digital products, affiliate marketing, online courses, and e-commerce. Construct a scalable web business that can take care of itself, connect with customers worldwide, and make money all the time. By utilizing innovation and technology, you may create a passive revenue stream that is both geographically and sustainably distributed.

6. Cultivating a Wealth Mindset

To reach your maximum potential for financial success, adopt a wealth mindset that is influenced by successful people like Elon Musk and Jeff Bezos. Have a positive financial mindset, be willing to take risks, and see failures as opportunities for growth. To attract prosperity and abundance into your life, make sure your thoughts, beliefs, and behaviors are in line with your financial objectives. Developing a wealth mindset paves the way for opportunity, growth, and the generation of passive income streams that help you reach financial independence.

7. Preservation of Wealth and Protection of Assets

To protect your assets and ensure your financial legacy, take a cue from Mark Zuckerberg and Bill Gates on how to preserve wealth. Protect your wealth from risks and uncertainties by putting strong asset protection mechanisms in place, such as insurance, trusts, and estate planning. Make sure your investments are diverse, guard against possible dangers, and build a long-lasting financial base. Your hard-earned wealth will continue to expand and benefit future generations if you prioritize asset protection and wealth preservation.

Chapter 10
Possessing An Abundance Mindset

Welcome to a life-changing adventure where your inner power of abundance will be revealed. In this riveting chapter, we delve into the concept of the abundance mindset—a attitude that can alter the way you approach opportunities, problems, and eventually, life itself. Using the experiences of the wealthiest people and visionaries on the planet as inspiration, we reveal seven essential techniques that will enable you to develop an abundant mindset and open the door to previously unheard-of levels of success. This section serves as your road map for reaching your full potential and opening up a world of endless possibilities, from changing your attitude to practicing gratitude.

---

1. ADOPT A GROWTH MENTALITY

Adopt a development mentality and learn from the successes of self-made millionaires such as Jeff Bezos and Oprah Winfrey. Consider challenges as opportunities for learning and progress rather than as barriers to overcome. Develop a mindset that is resilient to hardship and views failures as stepping stones to achievement. By having faith in your capacity to develop, adjust, and progress, you let yourself into a world of limitless opportunities and rapid expansion.

2. Every Day, Practice Gratitude

Aspiring businessmen like Tim Cook and Richard Branson should inspire you to live a life filled with thankfulness. Every day, set aside some time to consider how fortunate you are—from the possibilities that present themselves to the people you hold dear. You can attract more blessings and abundance into your life by cultivating an attitude of thankfulness, which changes your perspective from one of scarcity to abundance. Being grateful is an attitude that sets the stage for more success and happiness than it is merely an action.

3. Envision Your Achievement

To attract wealth into your life, use the technique of visualization, which visionaries like Elon Musk and Mark Cuban find effective. Conjure up a clear mental picture of your objectives, hopes, and desires, then lose yourself in the satisfaction and achievement that result from achieving them. You can direct your thoughts and actions toward accomplishing your goals by clearly and intentionally envisioning them. You can actualize your image of abundance by using visualization to increase your motivation, confidence, and drive.

4. Take Reasonable Chances

Take note of risk-taking trailblazers such as Elon Musk and Warren Buffett, and master the technique of taking measured risks. A mindset of plenty requires you to venture outside your comfort zone and take measured risks. Evaluate possibilities, balance risks and rewards, and make calculated risks that move you closer to your objectives. You may create opportunities for yourself and experience exponential growth by taking calculated risks with confidence and forethought.

5. Seek Fulfillment in Partnerships

Nurture abundance in your relationships, as relationship-centric leaders like Sheryl Sandberg and Bill Gates have done. Be in the company of upbeat, encouraging people who inspire and uplift you. Make deep connections, work with like-minded people, and look for mentors who can impart knowledge and insight. Building an abundance-minded community around you creates a positive ecosystem that supports your career and personal development.

6. Adopt a Wealthy Abundance Mentality

ADOPT AN ABUNDANCE mentality when it comes to riches to follow in the footsteps of successful businessmen like Jeff Bezos and Warren Buffett. Consider riches as an endless supply of opportunity rather than as a restricted resource. By thinking that you can attract wealth and create financial prosperity, you can change your perspective from one of scarcity to one of abundance. By adopting an abundant mindset when it comes to wealth, you create new opportunities for prosperity and financial success.

7. Reward via Increasing Abundance

Take inspiration from philanthropic trailblazers such as Bill and Melinda Gates on how to multiply plenty in your life via the transforming power of giving back. Giving and generosity are routes to abundance rather than merely being acts of compassion. Make a good impact on society and align with your values by supporting causes through charitable donations, volunteer work, or acts of service. Giving back with an open heart and an abundant spirit sets off a positive chain reaction that unexpectedly brings abundance back to you.

Bringing Wealth And Plenty In

1. Accept the Influence of Intention

The power of purpose is fundamental to drawing wealth and abundance. To draw money into your life, make sure that your feelings, ideas, and behaviors are all in line with your purpose. Take a cue from savvy businesspeople such as Richard Branson, whose steadfast intention brought him to unprecedented levels of success. You can invoke the law of attraction and attract abundance to you like a magnet by making a strong intention and carefully envisioning the results you want.

2. Develop an Attitude of Plenty

Change your perspective from one of scarcity to one of abundance. The wealthiest people in the world have adopted this important tactic. Turn your attention from constraints to opportunities, from scarcity to plenty. Take inspiration from individuals such as Jeff Bezos and Mark Zuckerberg, who tackle obstacles with an outlook that perceives possibilities everywhere. You may create an environment of wealth and boundless riches for yourself by cultivating an abundance attitude.

3. Execute Inspired Thoughts

The spark that ignites dreams into reality is inspired action. Take inspiration from forward-thinking businessmen like Bill Gates and Steve Jobs, who recognized the value of acting decisively and audaciously. Set objectives, make a strategy, and chase your aspirations without fear. You can send out a signal to the universe that you're ready to receive the abundance that is waiting for you by taking inspired action that is in line with your aspirations.

4. Make Being Grateful a Daily Ritual

THE PATH TO PLENTY is gratitude. Follow the lead of prosperous people, such as Tim Cook and Warren Buffett, who make thankfulness a regular part of their lives. Every day, set aside some time to express your thankfulness for all of life's blessings, large and little. When you are grateful, your attention is diverted from what is lacking to what is abundant, which allows additional blessings to pour into your life.

<hr/>

5. ESTABLISH PURPOSEFUL Networks

One should not undervalue the ability of networking to draw in prosperity. Take a cue from industry experts in networking, such as Sheryl Sandberg and Elon Musk, who use their relationships to propel their success. Seek out mentors who can provide knowledge and guidance, and surround yourself with people who encourage and support you. By purposefully networking and cultivating deep connections, you establish the environment conducive to prosperity.

6. Make an Investment in Ongoing Education

The wealthiest people on the planet are aware of the importance of lifelong learning and development. Take a cue from Oprah Winfrey and Jeff Bezos, who place a high value on learning new things. Make an investment in your professional and personal growth, look for fresh learning opportunities, and maintain your adaptability in a world that is changing quickly. Investing in ongoing education gives you the knowledge and abilities to draw wealth and abundance into your life.

7. Reward Others by Increasing Wealth

A key component of drawing wealth and abundance is philanthropy. Learn from the example of philanthropic luminaries such as Bill and Melinda Gates, who recognize the life-changing potential of charitable giving. Support causes that align with your values by volunteering, making charitable contributions, or performing acts of kindness. Giving back liberally and in an abundant manner causes a good energy chain reaction that increases your life's richness and prosperity.

Gratitude as a Wealth-Catalyst

1. Develop a Gratitude-Based Attitude

The discipline of developing an attitude of thankfulness is fundamental to drawing wealth. Take a cue from multibillionaire philanthropists such as Bill Gates and Mark Zuckerberg, who credit gratitude for a large portion of their achievements. You can attract money and prosperity by changing your attention from lack to abundance by recognizing and thanking the gifts in your life.

2. Utilize the Attraction Law

Gratitude is a strong magnet that draws your energy into alignment with the law of attraction. Embrace the mindset of prosperous businesspeople such as Elon Musk and Richard Branson, who recognize the significant influence of thankfulness in realizing their aspirations. Remaining grateful and concentrating on your blessings send a message to the universe that you are open to receiving more abundance in money.

3. Use the Visualization of Abundance.

When appreciation is added to visualization, it becomes an even more powerful technique for creating money. Take a cue from well-known executives who use visualization techniques in their daily lives, including Jeff Bezos and Tim Cook. Feel the joy and thankfulness that come with reaching your financial objectives while allowing yourself to experience the feelings that accompany achievement. You can establish a strong resonance with the riches you wish to attract by envisioning prosperity while feeling grateful.

4. Give to Show Your Gratitude

A foundational element of the appreciation mindset, giving is a means to greater prosperity. Take inspiration from philanthropic luminaries such as Bill Gates and Warren Buffett, who have demonstrated success via embracing the power of generosity. Contributing to worthy causes, being kind to others, or supporting philanthropic activities that you believe in increases the riches in your life. You generate a wealth-returning ripple effect when you distribute your plenty to others.

5. Keeping a gratitude journal

Maintaining a gratitude journal is an easy-to-use but powerful habit that can change your financial situation. Take a cue from well-known figures like Sheryl Sandberg and Oprah Winfrey, who credit gratitude journaling for a large portion of their success. Spend a few minutes every day listing three things for which you are thankful, emphasizing both material and immaterial gifts. You may attract more financial wealth and magnify the positive energy in your life by making journaling about thankfulness a habit.

6. Be in the company of gratitude

———⟫⬤⟨———

YOUR SURROUNDINGS HAVE a big impact on how you think and how much money you attract. Try to surround yourself with people who, like Sheryl Sandberg and Mark Zuckerberg, have a mindset of thankfulness. Participate in collective appreciation exercises, exchange tales of plenty, and support one another during times of thankfulness. Embracing an attitude of gratitude allows you to build a network of people who encourage prosperity and financial growth.

7. Being Grateful on a Daily Basis

Make it a non-negotiable habit to include thankfulness in your everyday activities. Follow the lead of prosperous businessmen like Elon Musk and Jeff Bezos, who begin each day by expressing thanks. Start your day with a gratitude walk in the outdoors, a gratitude meditation, or thankfulness affirmations. You may create a great vibe for the day and allow prosperity and abundance to come into your life by starting the day with an attitude of appreciation.

Conclusion Chapter
A Matter Of Emergency

Precious one, before you drop this book, I intend to address the most important issue both in time and eternity. It is a matter of life after death. It is a matter of your soul. All I want you to know is:

1. **Life is terminal.**

"And as it is appointed unto men once to die, but after this the judgment": (Hebrews 9:27)

Everyone on earth has an appointment with death. No one lives forever. You are dust and must one day return to the dust of the earth. And your spirit would have to return to God as well.

"Then shall the dust return to the earth as it was: and the spirit shall return unto God who gave it". (Ecclesiastes 12:7)

The thing here is that, death is not the end of life. Life stills continues after death either in heaven or hell.

"And many of them that sleep in the dust of the earth shall awake, some to everlasting life, and some to shame and everlasting contempt." Daniel 12:2

1. **There is life after death.**

The life after death is either with God in heaven or with Satan in hell. People who are not born again, Will be turned to hell fire with Satan as their master. How do I know this?

"The wicked shall be turned into hell, and all the nations that forget God." (Psalm 9:17)

Heaven is a place for only those who have their names written in the lamp's book – those who are born again

And there shall in no wise enter into it any thing that defileth, neither whatsoever worketh abomination, or maketh a lie: but they which are written in the Lamb's book of life. (Revelation 21:27)

1. How you live in time, determines where you will end in eternity

" Let us hear the conclusion of the whole matter: Fear God, and keep his commandments: for this is the whole duty of man. For God shall bring every work into judgment, with every secret thing, whether it be good, or whether it be evil." (Ecclesiastes 12:13-14)

1. Who you live for now determines who you will be with in eternity.

Who you live for determines who you will live with in eternity. Does your life please God or Satan?

"Jesus saith unto him, I am the way, the truth, and the life: no man cometh unto the Father, but by me." (John 14:6)

You must understand that there no salvation in any religion but Jesus the son of God.

"Neither is there salvation in any other: for there is none other name under heaven given among men, whereby we must be saved." (Acts 4:12)

1. Live with eternity in view.

Do you really know your end? Where are you going after death? Who will you live with in eternity? Who are you living for, right now? Does God know you as His Own?

"Nevertheless the foundation of God standeth sure, having this seal, The Lord knoweth them that are his. And, Let every one that nameth the name of Christ depart from iniquity." (2 Timothy 2:19).

To help you answer all the above questions with certainty, accept Jesus as your lord and savior.

Pray this prayer:

Lord Jesus, I come to you today to surrender my life completely to you. Forgive me of all the self-centred life I lived. I am sorry for all. Lord, have mercy on me. Receive me today as your child. Lord Jesus, I accept you today as my lord and saviour. Dear Holy Spirit come into my heart. Fill me and control me. Write my name in the book of life. Remove my name from the book of death. From today forward ever, backward never. Thank you for saving me. Amen. Locate a Bible believing Church and get yourself planted. If you are in WA, you can join us at the GGGC Seers Chapel, Right behind Islamic Hospital /Girls SHS., , Airstrip, wa.

For Partnership, Testimonies and other enquiry please call:

+233245224028/+233209066380

Or write via

milsthomass@gmail.com

You can also join the company of great publishers by supporting this worthy cause financially. Send your seed to momo account:+233(0)24 522 4028 /+233(0)20 906 6380.

God bless you!

Don't miss out!

Visit the website below and you can sign up to receive emails whenever Thomas Mills publishes a new book. There's no charge and no obligation.

https://books2read.com/r/B-A-TWSFC-BRESE

Connecting independent readers to independent writers.

Also by Thomas Mills

2
How To Become The Best Of Men And Access The Best Of Life:
From Ordinationary To Exceptional The Path Of Men Who Thrive.
Vol 2

Standalone
Financial Freedom In 5 Month: Waging War Against Poverty
How to Set Effective Financial Goals: From Dreams to Dollars A
Guide to Financial Freedom